Inter Culture
ASSOCIATES
BOX 277–THOMPSON, CONNECTICUT 06277

JAYAPRAKASH
Rebel Extraordinary

Jayaprakash
Rebel Extraordinary

Dr. Lakshmi Narain Lal

INDIAN BOOK COMPANY
NEW DELHI

Published by India Book Company, 36-C, Connaught Place,
New Delhi 110001 and printed at Daawn Printing Works,
2624, Nicholson, Phase-I, New Delhi 110032.

PRINTED IN INDIA

Published by Indian Book Company, 36 C, Connaught Place,
New Delhi 110001 and printed at Dhawan Printing Works,
26-A, Mayapuri, Phase I, New Delhi 110027

PRINTED IN INDIA

To

J.P.

who inspired a revolution

Introduction

TWO years ago, I visited Mithila with my friend, Shivsagar Mishra, and we utilised this trip to see a lot of Bihar. Back in Patna immediately after, I met Sri Jitendra Singh, Special Correspondent of the *Times of India* in that city, and it was through him that I first met Jayaprakashji. We talked a little about literature and politics and very little else. The next day, Jayaprakashji invited me to tea, and on this second meeting, I was completely captivated.

I still had no thought about writing a book. But a few days after I returned to Delhi, Professor Bimal Prasad suggested, in passing, that I write about J.P.'s life. A few days later, Dinkarji echoed this suggestion, and whenever I mentioned the possibility to friends, they were encouraging. Nevertheless, I was sceptical, and I put the thought out of my head.

Soon after J.P. invited me to visit him in Musehari. I went, flattered, curious; but it is difficult to describe how impressed I was with the work of Sarvodaya in this Naxalite stronghold. Suddenly it seemed important that this biography be written. I discussed it with J.P. and asked for his blessings.

He said: 'You must read all the literature about Gandhiji and Vinobaji before you begin', and he gave me his blessings and consent.

As I delved deeper into the founts of his life, it became astonishingly clear that I was writing about a great and uni-

7

que individual. With increasing trepidation but immense pleasure. I persevered, and this book emerged.

The guiding spirit behind this task, from start to finish, has been Professor Bimal Prasad. I cannot find words to express my infinite gratitude. Among many others, too numerous to list, are Mahavir Prasad Sinha, A.C. Sen and Dr. Haridev Sharma.

A mass of material, accessible to the scholar, exists in any good library. J.P. himsetf has been a prolific writer, and every stage of his career is punctuated by a spate of letters, theses and pamphlets. About his private life, however, J.P. has written hardly anything, and it has been a struggle to keep this book from being a mere chronicle of his public involvements.

Among the many works and documents which deal with the early Socialist organisation, I have found Benipuri's book and the records of the *Janata* particularly useful. I am grateful to Sri B.P. Sinha for making these available. For the Sarvodaya period, I am indebted to J.P.'s colleague, Sri Sachchidanand, whose guidance and private collection have been of immense value. I must also acknowledge the help extended by three young Sarvodaya workers, Prabhas Joshi, Anupam Mishra and Shravan Kumar Garg. To Dinkar, who is with us no more, I express my gratitude and homage.

This list would not be complete without the names of Sri B.R. Nanda, Sri Dharmavir and Dr. Sharma of the Nehru Memorial Museum Library. My typist, Sri Bhim Singh Negi deserves thanks for an onerous duty.

And to my wife, who has patiently and lovingly supported my pre-occupation with this work, I will always be indebted.

LAKSHMI NARAIN LAL

Chapter One

THE first thing you notice about Jayaprakash Narayan is his utter simplicity. J.P. is such an 'ordinary' man. His dress, his life style, even his books, attest to his naturalness. Where was the fierce individualist I had heard about? Where was the politician who had no need of a following to bolster his convictions? ... There is something sad and tired about his face. Somehow, his quiet, gentle visage must co-exist with an inner fire.

J.P. does not allow you to draw too close, to peer behind his persona. Politely, he keeps you at a little distance. There is a threshold of intimacy you cannot cross. And yet, somehow, he manages to project the impression that you have a special, close relationship with him.

Only for a single person did J.P. drop his defences—Prabhavati, his wife. She was a window into J.P. There is no other way of fathoming his depth or leaning into his soul. Through the story of their life together, one learns that J.P.'s mystique rests on a solid plank of empathy and kindness. Once this is perceived, even his irascibility is explained. A blend of cold intellect and fervid emotion co-exists in the same man.

In the face he turns to the world, he bears the marks of a relentless crusader. Once he decides that a cause is just and right, his involvement becomes total, unflinching. All other distractions are subordinate and are swept aside. One consequence of this nature of J.P.'s involvements is that no single doctrine, no single school of thought, no institution has been

able to claim him as solely its own : "When people submit
to closed systems of thought, they develop 'ideological blink-
ers'. They cannot then think freely. Today, I am not a
member of any Party. Though I am part of the Sarvodaya
movement, I am in no way imprisoned by its outlook. I am
free to change my mind."

J.P.'s political individualism has earned him many enemies,
many taunts :

'J.P. enjoys the various disguises he can assume through
his political writings.'

'He always stumbles at the critical moment.'

'In the race for office, J.P. has always backed the wrong
horse.'

'J.P. has become a reformist, he is no longer a revolutionary.'

Fundamentally, however, these remarks do not touch the heart
of the matter. During the *gramdan* and *bhoodan* movements,
and now, in the mid-seventies, in the midst of the movement
in Bihar, J.P.'s work lies in the rural areas. On his way from
one village to another, he is often mobbed by huge crowds
of people, eagerly pressing forward their sorrows and problems for his attention. He belongs to that rare breed of men
in whom each supplicant sees a messiah of his own—a man
of whom the politicians think : "He will make me a minister."
To a poor farmer, he is the Collector, come to restore his
land to him. Another farmer runs up to him and says,
"*Sarkar*, there is no water in my fields." A worker takes J.P.
for a "comrade" who will fight for his rights. A housewife
asks him to persuade her run-away husband to return to her.
And to the throng of children, J.P. is a magical figure, a *baba*,
who will bless the village and cause an aeroplane to land in
the village square . . . . And thus, he is many things to many
people.

The landless and the exploited Nagas found a champion
in him. Sheikh Abdulla saw in him a friend and sympathiser.
The dacoits of the Chambal valley trusted him. And lately,
he has become a father-figure and guru to whole communities of turbulent and restless students in the country. Among
the political figures of post-Independence India, J.P. has
surely been unique— *babaji*, a man concerned about his

reputation, about being above the spoils of office.

This is an important insight into J.P.'s character. He sees himself as a family elder. Family and society—a difference of magnitude. His concern for values and principles, for social morality, is filial and militant. And as a result, his plane of thought and action has been both moral and political. And it is difficult to crystallise moral concern in office.

It is impossible, however, to explain his simplicity and spontaneity. Here again, he is unlike Gandhi. Gandhi had to struggle hard against some of the traits he had acquired early in life. His life-style, even his dress, became consciously ascetic : an ordinary, nondescript boy became an extraordinary man. J.P.'s development was, in a sense, in reverse. He transformed extraordinary beginnings into a natural simplicity. He *became* ordinary.

J.P.'s politics are founded on a belief in the effectiveness of struggle. Movements are born and movements die, but struggle born of political awareness reaches beyond its immediate goals, engages in a fundamental questioning of accepted truths. And yet, whenever he has seen the dimensions of a "conflict" shrink and gorge itself upon its own vitals, J.P. has not hesitated to free himself of such an allegiance, regardless of whether the commitment was to a Marxist, "Congress Socialist", or P.S.P. programme. Those who stayed behind have called him fickle, an opportunist, an individualist, a reformist. But these taunts have always rebounded on those who uttered them, and behind all their bitterness is a deep regret that they have lost a great leader.

Another trait : J.P. is that rare individual who has not grown old hating this world, curling up in moral indignation at what surrounds him. It is a sensibility that he seems to have acquired from Gandhi. His love encompasses the criminal, the dacoit, the adversary, the Naxalite, regardless. For their just causes J.P. would even risk his very life.

J.P. is not a man of sentiment. He is a man of imagination, of idealism, which is quite a different thing. Sentiment is soon exhausted ; it feeds on itself, it is intermittent. It also breeds a certain indifference towards more concrete issues. But imagination and idealism never die.

Imagination ! Idealism ! For what ? For equality, freedom
and fraternity. For their sake J.P. has been to jail. He has
watched as freedom turned into ashes. He has pulled out all
his stakes and prepared to fight his battle alone. His main-
stay has always been an instinctive faith that although man
cannot attain absolute perfection, he can advance, by slow
degrees, towards truth.

For Gandhi, truth was God. For J.P., truth is less an end
in itself than a powerful catalyst, a leavening yeast, but never
a 'deity'. Truth is an essential part of a quest for a 'new
man', a quest of faith.

Where does J.P. derive this inexhaustible faith from ?

As a young man, like a lot of his fellow students, J.P. was an
ardent nationalist. Behind his belief was a predilection for
revolutionary methods of winning freedom. When Gandhiji
caught the imagination of the country with his first *satyagraha*,
J.P. had not yet hardened into a revolutionary. He was swept
up by this rising tide into a breathless, rarefied atmosphere
that left its stamp on him for the rest of his life. The possibility that three could be 'moral' politics, a goal other than
power and authority, quickly lifted him out of his conventional
revolutionary mould.

When J.P. returned from America, the nationalist movement had picked up momentum. J.P. immediately jumped
into the fray, and involved himself in the struggle with all his
energy. He saw, however, that the communists were holding
back, refraining from participating in what they called a
'bourgeois' movement. J.P. was aghast, and bitterly assailed
this line.

Soon after, he dissociated himself from the communists, and
became a nationalist cadet. Already, by this time, independence
and *swarajya* had acquired a meaning considerably beyond the
narrow sense of the term, A free India had come to mean a
socialist India. Together with some of his colleagues who
shared his views, he formed the Congress Socialist Party. A
time came when the Communist Party and the C.S.P. joined
hands and worked out a strategy together. But their brittle
union was completely shattered by the news of Stalin's
atrocities in the U.S.S.R., which the communists could not

bring themselves to condemn.

Once again, J.P. was forced to examine the fundamental tenets of Marxism. The Russian case furnished a concrete example of Marxism in practice. J.P. studied the antecedents of Marxism in European Socialism, and its limitations when transplanted to an Asiatic soil. Finally, he had to confront two crucial questions : the question of the 'means' (the route towards a Marxist society) and the concept of materialism and the place of morality. Commitment to liberty-equality-fraternity—the very goals that had led J.P. towards universal scientific socialism—now ushered him towards Gandhi :

If man and his consciousness and the society and culture which he has built up are mere manifestations of matter—howsoever dialectically active—I can see no reason why in such a society, anyone should try to be good, that is, be generous, kind and unselfish. Why should one then feel sympathy with those who are weak, poor or sick ? What is if matter will dissolve into matter after death ? So what incentive can there be for moral behaviour ? . . .

It is fundamental to J.P. that an ethical view of the world, of human thought and action, flow out of any attempt to make sense of the way society works. "Whosoever experiences this total view will adopt a moral code as naturally as he would breathe."

It was after Independence that J.P. tried to concretise the philosophy and vision that lay behind Gandhi's conception of the Lok Sevak Sangh. The same principles influenced his own *jeevandan*. It is from here that we can trace that faith, that moral sensibility that is J.P.'s individual contribution to Indian politics. The 'individual' is a construct of Western cultural notions and experience. In contrast, Indian thought conceptualises 'man' i.e. *manushya*. Whereas the individual is seen to be autonomous and self-motivated, *manushya* is not free. He has *karma*, acts and duties to perform, and only through these does he attain freedom. Having 'become' free, he strives for *mukti* i.e. salvation. Here, we encounter a real difficulty in Indian thought, a dangerous chasm that separates man from society. Where man's personal salvation alone motivates his actions, society becomes irrelevant. Shutting his eyes to society, he contemplates a shore that lies beyond it; he runs away from a creative confrontation with it. He imagines himself to be outside society.

J.P. believes that man, as Indian civilisation sees him, is an abstraction, an unreal thing. The individual is a mere manifestation of this abstraction. Man is an individual. It is impossible to contemplate man outside society. He has no meaning and no relevance outside society.

J.P. fuses the two concepts, man and individual, to arrive at his own solution. Man realises himself only when, as an individual, he engages in struggle. Though struggle is directed outwards, it results in inner change. Interacting with other men, defining a goal, struggling towards it, recognising that one's actions can change the world—these pave the way towards realisation.

Nowhere has J.P. actually spelled out this view. He does not need to, because he is *living* the idea, explicating it in every action. He proclaims the concept through *jeevandan*, through his mission to the Chambal valley dacoits and his endless journeys on foot through the villages.

The same view is evident in his pronouncements : 'Our party system attempts to reduce the people to sheep, whose only function is to choose shepherds at the appointed time . . . . In such a system, I do not see that freedom, for which I and the people of this country fought.'

J.P. is at his best when he is involved in struggle. The image of his as a man singing *hari kirtan* (devotional songs) is utterly false. He is himself only in the fray. What he looks for in other men is a sign that they are people who will struggle with him, shoulder to shoulder. If he urges involvement, it is because he is completely involved himself.

By tying himself up, he frees himself.

He attains peace through struggle.

After Prabhavati's death recently, J.P. has changed so much. Physically, he is old and frail. But his mind seems charged with youth and vitality. A *satyagrahi* again.

Strolling with him on the lawns of Delhi, a frightening thought crosses my mind. The foundations of society cannot be *satya*, truth—they can only be non-violent. And, truth is frightening. The poverty of Saharsa village, the tempestuous youth of Musehari, the dacoits of the Chambal valley, Tibet, Nagaland wanting to secede, Kashmir, Pakistan, Bangladesh—these are all truths. What they tell us is: you must destroy your antiquated beliefs, the status quo, and pull out your faith by the roots. What will remain thereafter ?

This is what J.P. wants to know.

This is the burdensome question that he has hoisted on to his old shoulders and hawks on the streets, in valley and dale, throughout the country:

Is there a single example, in history, of a social revolution that has successfully achieved what it set out to do ? Look at the French Revolution, its objectives—liberty, equality, fraternity. Look at the Russian Revolution—at Lenin's promise that after the revolution, all Soviets would be in the hands of workers, soldiers and peasants.

Violent revolutions always give way to one form of dictatorship or another. For this reason, after a revolution, a new ruling class emerges out of the chaos, the masses once again become slaves. That is why I say that violence does not right a wrong situation, and the people have been given the wrong impression.

And so, a leader of a violent revolutionary cadre now preaches the light of non-violent revolution in the dirty, dusty villages of the country. He is misunderstood. Some people call him a misguided revolutionary. They see him engaged in utterly futile idealism. They ask him, 'J.P. ! why have you retired to an insignificant corner of political life ?' He has replied, 'The whole thing is so new and untried, it is impossible to explain clearly. But my work will speak for itself . . .'

As the world has changed, in knowledge, experience, potential, J.P. has devised new methods of struggle. The very notion of freedom has expanded and acquired the dimensions a previous generation could not have visualised. The weapons in the struggle for such a freedom have also to be refashioned, their efficacy carefully estimated.

Gandhi once summed up the essential message of all his political and social work: every man, however small, is capable of realising himself, and in this small way, of contributing towards a social revolution. The first person to grasp its significance was Ram Manohar Lohia. And J.P. has tried to translate this message into his own life's work.

Had I said that there was another Jayaprakash Narayan that Prabhavati allowed us to glimpse ?

Jayaprakash and Prabha were married while they were still children. Barely two years after their marriage, J.P. left for the United States of America to study. Prabha, left behind, joined Gandhi's *ashram* and observed *brahmacharya*.

Seven years later, when J.P. returned, they began to live together ; but Prabha's vow of *brahmacharya* and her involvement with Gandhi's programme caused its stresses. In the relationship between husband and wife, there remained an empty space that needed to be mapped and filled in. But how ?

Prabhavati's was the easier task. In addition to the attributes of Indian womanhood, she had the experience of Gandhi's moral universe to steady her resolve. *Ahimsa* and *satyagraha* were twin postulates, and her commitment to the ideal (and the means to attain it) was unfaltering. Jayaprakash, too, had his beliefs, but they were not easily applicable to a personal and intimate relationship. His intellectual bias was Western: rationalism was an unfailing yardstick, dialectical materialism a tenet.

Thus—two persons, together, yet set apart. Different, yet man and wife. Where was the meeting ground ? Time and patience were needed before either could give himself to the other. And yet, this too, for Prabhavati was easy, for Jayaprakash difficult.

On the public platform, Jayaprakash would tirade against Gandhi, subjecting his arguments to a searching scrutiny. Behind him, on the same platform, Prabhavati quietly spun raw cotton on a *charkha*. For her, belief in Gandhi, and utter devotion to a man who opposed Gandhi's creed was not a contradiction.

And J.P. was a complete atheist and an opponent of Gandhi's . . . . Husband and wife were poles apart !

In 1937, there came a brief period of stability in J.P.'s life, when he decided to work for the Congress Socialist Party and make Patna his headquarters. Before that, as the General Secretary of the Party, J.P. had to make frequent trips to

Bombay and Varanasi (Benares). Prabhavati moved about in Gandhi's following. Occasionally, husband and wife would be together. They would stay with J.P.'s sister in Patna. But it was not till 1937 that J.P. rented a house and summoned Prabhavati from the *ashram* at Wardha. What a strange household that was ! Prabhavati was most at home in Gandhi's *ashram*. Even then when J.P. was away for long stretches of time, she took the opportunity to be with Bapu whenever she could.

Temperamentally, Prabhavati was devoted and loving. Absolute devotion to Bapu had become almost a religious duty. Yet, she lavished the same kind of care on whomever she was with—in Srinagar (Bihar), on her mother; in Sitab Diyara, on her father-in-law; and in Patna, on her husband.

Occasionally, at their house in Patna, Prabhavati, Jayaprakash and Ganga Babu were all together. They lived on a shoestring budget. Prabhavati did all the housework, even though those were times of conflict. Jayaprakash was a staunch socialist, Prabhavati, a Gandhian. J.P. would make fun of Prabha's *charkha*. He would taunt her about reading the *Gita* every day. For Prabhavati, these activities were part of her *dharma*. To J.P., they were merely opiates.

In their views and their attitudes to life, they were utterly unlike one another. Yet there was a strong emotional bond that held them together.

Long ago, Gandhi had told J.P. that Prabha would stick to her resolve of *brahmacharya*. 'You can marry someone else if you wish.'

Greatly troubled, J.P. replied, 'Bapu, how can you say that ? How can you say such a harsh thing ?'

The difficulties of mutual adjustment remained with them. Bapu wrote regularly :

Dear Prabha

  Why did you write such a sad letter ? Everyone has his own beliefs. Why are you so worried ? Life is so short. There is so much uncertainty. All that remains is dharma, *which is embedded in truth and* ahimsa. *Live your ideals; express them in new ways.*

Prabhavati talked about the future in a letter to J.P.,

'Whenever I see Kishor Lal Bhai and Gomti Behen, I wonder when God will give us an opportunity to be together. What could be a greater wish than that we should live and work together ?' And, in another letter: 'We should try and forget our differences. If we want to serve the poor, we have to be prepared to make sacrifices.'

J.P. has said, 'If I did not have such a deep regard for Bapu, life would have become intolerably difficult for her' (Prabha).

Bapu once asked Prabha, 'You will take my place, won't you ?' 'How can I replace you, Bapu,' Prabha replied. 'I don't have your knowledge, no special accomplishments or virtues.' Bapu burst out laughing and patted her on the back. 'You are silly,' he said. 'Why do you need wisdom to take my place ? You need only four things—love, devotion, sacrifice . . .' He did not pronounce the fourth word.

'Write them down for me, Bapu', Prabha said.

Bapu wrote the four words on a scrap of paper and handed it to Prabha. 'Don't tell anyone about this. Keep it to yourself,' he said softly.

When Prabha left the Aga Khan's palace, the government officials did not allow her to take certain things with her. One of them was this chit of paper. Many years later, Prabhavati said, 'The Government took away my greatest treasure. I don't recall what the fourth word was.'

In fact, that fourth word was *Jayaprakash*. The Hindu wife never articulates her husband's name; she cannot remember it, for to remember a person's name, you need to be aware of a separate identity, of being a different person.

'Don't tell anyone about this. Keep it to yourself.' The secret remained with Prabha. And when she passed away she became a part of Jayaprakash. She is still there, evident in the way he lives, and talks.

Chapter Two

FROM the point where the river Ganga flows out of Uttar Pradesh into Bihar, in Shahabad district, and until it drops into Purnea in West Bengal, the mighty river creates large mud embankments midstream. The villagers call these tiny islands *diyaras*. They are, in fact, just like marine islands. All around them, huge expanses of water. And cloistered away from the sucking tides, the villages are built on these islands, green and full. The *diyaras* are strange places—and even stranger are their inhabitants. They are fair and sturdy, sentimental, and easily roused. Aggressive with huge, powerful arms, and endless talkers, they are a self-respecting and proud people. On the nutritious diet of bread, rice and buffalo's milk, their sons are already men at the age of seventeen. If you really want to see fine specimen of men, visit the *diyaras*.

Sitab Diyara is a special little mound. The old folks of the village say the settlement was founded by Raja Sitabrai, who during the last years of Muslim supremacy, had been the *subedar* (governor) of Bihar. At a critical moment in history, the *subedar* forsook his Muslim overlords, and hitched his star to the East India Company. Before he died, he had helped to lay the foundations of British rule in Bihar.

It is a strange irony of fate that, in the same village which Sitabrai founded, there was born a boy who spent the best years of his life fighting British colonialism.

Sitab Diyara has a unique terrain. Near the village, the

19

river Saryu (Ghaghra) becomes a tributary of the Ganga. This is also the place where the boundary between the States of Uttar Pradesh and Bihar is demarcated—on paper, that is. The shifting courses of the two rivers do their utmost to obliterate this boundary. The people of Sitab Diyara are never sure whether they are in Bihar or the two rivers have pushed them into the neighbouring State.

J.P. has a faint memory of his early boyhood days. He says, 'At that time, our village was in the grip of a plague epidemic. We had some land in Ballia district of Uttar Pradesh, about two and a half miles west of the village, in an area called Babarbani. Because of the plague, our family had moved there. That was where I was born.'

Sitab Diyara is not just a nondescript little village. In fact, it is a *kasbah*, midway between a village and a town, with a population of forty thousand. All of Bihar's most typical castes are represented in Sitab Diyara. They live in *tolas*, or wards ; and mostly men of the same caste live together in each *tola*. The largest *tola* is inhabited by Kayasthas and, in popular parlance, is known as Lala Tola. All Kayasthas there belong to the sub-caste of Srivastava. Perhaps, they came here from Sravasti. This does not mean that they are all from Oudh (Avadh). Many of them are from Bareilly and Delhi. Kayasthas are traditionally scribes and writers. But the Kayasthas of Sitab Diyara pride themselve not only on their intellectual capacities, but on the strength of their arms as well. Unlike the Kayasthas' traditional image, these Kayasthas are people who also live by hard physical labour.

There once lived in Lala Tola a person named Babu Devki Nandan Lal. He was an Inspector of Police, a fearless and influential man. The story goes that a Superintendent of Police, an Englishman, once insulted Devki Babu, upon which he beat up the Superintendent with a club. It was a criminal offence. But the Englishman swallowed his pride and kept quiet. Whom could he tell—without looking foolish—that a "native" had beaten him up ?

Devki Babu had no children. Preoccupied with his own power and status, he felt no grievous loss at this. But his wife spent all her time in sadness, longing for a child. Ultimately, she visited a famous *baba* (holy man) in Shahabad, Harsu

Brahmababa, and with his blessings, a son was born, who was named Harsood Pal.

Like his father, Harsood too was given an English-language education. Temperamentally, however, he was totally unlike Devki Nandan. Later in life, he rose from the position of *ziladar* to that of a Revenue Assistant. A very simple, straightforward, saintly man, he cultivated none of the vices typical of the petty official. He was kind and sympathetic, taciturn and simple. His wife was called Phoolrani—a picture of kindness and love. She spoke very little and lived a simple, saintly life. This woman was Jayaprakash's mother.

Harsood Pal and Phoolrani had six children, of whom. Jayaprakash was the fourth. Three brothers and three sisters. The eldest was Hari Prakash, who died of cholera at the age of thirteen. Three years later, the eldest daughter, Chandrabhanu, also died, when she was only eleven.

J.P. was born in the beginning of the twentieth century. It was a time of great change, when mankind was awakening to the possibility of exchanging old ideas for new ones. Cultural change, equality, socialism, freedom—these words came to have a new meaning now. The nineteenth century had already witnessed a great awakening among the Indian people. Now, this energy was to be channelled into political awareness.

At the beginning of the twentieth century, a number of thinkers drew attention to the relationship between cultural tradition and political sovereignty. Men like Tilak, Aurobindo, Gokhale and Gandhi were not merely political leaders. They were men steeped in Indian culture, their political consciousness emanating from a new awareness of India's cultural heritage. All over Asia, countries underwent a similar awakening to their own identity. China, Japan, Egypt, Turkey, Arabia, Iran—the same tide swept through all of them. The new mood signalled a clash with colonial domination and imperialism.

But it was also a time of false bravado, of symbolic but meaningless acts. In Poona, in Ayodhya, the statues of Queen Victoria were disfigured. In Calcutta, the Commissioner was assassinated, in Allahabad the Collector was shot. These were terrorist acts. They amounted to little and made very little difference. They were emotional outbursts.

One day, Jayaprakash's mother became concerned about him.
She had noticed that he was not as active as other children
of his age. His speech seemed retarded. He walked very
gingerly, as though he was weighing each step before he
placed it on the ground. He tried to talk, but he had not cut
a tooth yet. He could only gurgle. His mother was worried.
'*Arre* ! Why haven't his milk teeth appeared yet ? Is he a
baul ?' Baul ! The name stuck. Even today, his family members and intimate friends call him Baulji.

Jayaprakash's father worked in the Irrigation Department. He
spent most of his time in Shahabad district, which was later
sub-divided into Rohtas and Ara. Baulji lived with his parents
in Shahabad city. No sign of his later penchant for struggle
was evident at this age. He was strangely quiet and composed.
No jumping around, running here and there. No naughtiness.
No games, no toys.

Babu Harsood Pal would listen to other people comment
on his son's strange behaviour: '*Huzoor*, Babua behaves as
though he is always in deep thought.' 'Yes. God knows what
he keeps thinking about.' One day he said to Phoolrani. 'He
is not a little boy. He is an old man.'

Later in life, political associates would resent the way J.P.
talked to them — as though they mere children before him.

It was now time for Baulji to go to school. The quicker a
Kayastha boy learns to wield the pen, the better. J.P. does
recall bits of his childhood : 'As a child, I was very influenced
by the love, the simplicity and tenderness that I found in my
mother. My father too, was pleasant, but he was a somewhat
distant figure. I do not remember him as clearly as I do my
mother. He maintained a certain reserve.'

J.P.'s mother went with her husband to whichever place
his work took him. There were times when Baulji was left in the
care of his grandmother.

Sitab Diyara had one primary school. One of the teachers
attached to the school, who was also a wrestler, used to come
to the house and teach J.P. He even lived there for a while.
That early instruction was a good influence on Baulji. The
teacher was also somewhat of a nationalist, and some of this

rubbed off on the boy. This lasted only a short while, after which Jayaprakash went to schools in the various places where his father was posted.

One day, his father brought home a pair of pigeons. It was an unusually hot summer. One of the birds got heat-stroke and died, and Baulji was tremendously upset. He did not eat for two days. Baulji was very fond of animals. He was particularly fond of deer, dogs and rabbits. The family had a mare at home, that gave birth to a little colt. One day, Baulji took something to eat for the colt. For some reason, the mare kicked Baulji, hurting him quite badly. After this incident, his father wanted to get rid of the mare, but the boy refused to let him do so.

Another incident of those days is connected with a man named Aditya Mishra who used to come to the house to tutor Baulji. The father noticed that Mishra was not doing a good job of teaching the boy, and asked the tutor to leave. Once again the boy refused to let his father do anything of the kind. The tutor stayed on for a while longer.

After his primary education, Baulji was sent to the capital city of Bihar, Patna. Having lived all his life in villages and towns it was like entering the big, wide world for him. He was to live with Shambhusharanji. Technically, Shambhusha-ranji was a nephew of Baulji's. But he was much older, and at the time that the nephew was studying in college to become a lawyer, the uncle began his school career.

Patna of those days bore no resemblance at all to what it looks like now. The streets were not broad and paved. No cars, buses, trains. Just gigs and *tumtums*, horse-tandems. In the centre of the town, an ancient building housed the Patna Collegiate School. The first breath of nationalist feeling had already touched this institution. The Headmaster was a man named Amjad Ali Khan, a fine teacher, who, apart from studies, believed in developing the character of the boys. It was time for Baulji to become Jayaprakash Narayan to his friends. His name is entered in the school records for the seventh standard.

Baulji's style of dress changed now. He wore a flat-cap, a shirt and coat, a dhoti and English shoes. He was about twelve or thirteen years old. But for his age, he was exceptionally quiet and serious—and hardworking.

The school did not have a proper hostel, but a building (that exists even today) called Sarasvati Bhavan, was utilised for that purpose. Jayaprakash stayed here. At the time, this building was an important meeting place for Patna's student leaders. Bihar's most famous political figures had lived here. Anugraha Babu, Ramcharita Sinha, Raghunandan Pande had studied there. Rajendra Prasad, free India's first President, Ram Naumi Babu, a *satyagrahi* with Gandhi at Champaran, and the famous Sri Babu, had stayed there.

These lads were not only exceptional students ; they were all, in some sense, influenced by the rising tide of nationalist feeling. They would have meetings at Sarasvati Bhavan and tell tales of freedom fighters. The country's problems would be discussed. Nationalist literature would be smuggled into the building, and surreptitiously passed from hand to hand. The atmosphere of the Bhavan had a great influence on young Jayaprakash. Suddenly, his horizon extended beyond the closed world of school texts. Newsletters, pamphlets, nationalist books—the whole world opened up for the precocious boy.

One of Jayaprakash's classmates stole his books. He knew who had done it, but he had not seen it actually happen. What was he to do ? After a while, the Headmaster found out about the matter, and had the books returned to Jayaprakash. The latter went and begged forgiveness of the boy for putting him to shame. In turn, the boy was so overwhelmed by Jayaprakash's kindness, that he confessed all his previous misdemeanours.

J.P. recalls another small incident. He was struggling with an arithmetical problem. The solution in the textbook was wrong. He got so involved with the problem that he skipped his meals. Finally, he worked out the answer. But when it was time to go to bed, he pulled the sheet over his head and started crying. It was late at night, and he suddenly became aware of hunger pangs. Jayaprakash still recalls the difficulty with which he slept on an empty stomach that night.

Soon after, his eldest sister, Chandravati, got married. Her husband, Braj Bihari Sahay, worked at the High Court in Patna, and Jayaprakash moved out of Sarasvati Bhavan to stay with them. Until he left Patna, this was the place where he stayed. By a strange coincidence, Braj Bihari was a man closely akin to Jayaprakash's father Harsood Pal. Calm and good-natured, he had a decisive influence on the impressionable boy.

Jayaprakash's school was quite a distance away from the High Court living quarters. He received three annas as his daily allowance. Out of this, he spent one anna going to school by *tumtum*. Lunch cost him another anna. And the remainder he paid to the *tumtumwallah* for the return journey.

About this time, the Collegiate School got a new Head-master, a man named Ras Masood, who later became the Education Minister to the Nizam of Hyderabad, and received a knighthood. Jayaprakash was busy preparing for the entrance exams to High School. His English, Hindi and Sanskrit were sound and his arithmetic was excellent. It seemed as though an inclination towards the arts was balanced by a precise, mathematical mind.

Ras Masood was replaced by Whitmore Sahib. An insensitive man, Whitmore had scheduled an examination on a festival day. Jayaprakash and five friends got together to protest. On the day of the examination, these six students absented themselves. Whitmore was furious. Next day, he summoned the absentees to his chamber.

'Why were all of you not at the examination?'

'Yesterday was a holiday.'

'What for ?'

'*Puja.*'

'Quiet ! Put your hands out. I am going to cane you.'

The six of them put out their hands without hesitation. The Headmaster was amazed. But he went ahead and caned them.

This was Jayaprakash's first lesson in protest.

It was already dark in the school quadrangle. The other students had already left. Outside the schoolhouse, the ground was uneven and slushy. Earlier, there had been a lot of rain. Slipping and falling, Jayaprakash walked a considerable distance until he found a *tumtum*. He put his right hand into his pocket to look for something. His palm was swollen, and his fingers felt lifeless. As he walked on, he recalled Whitmore Sahib's angry red face. This was the moment when Jayaprakash perhaps first realised that life was strewn with pitfalls and dangers. It was not enough to be straightforward and simple.

In 1919, Jayaprakash stood first in the High School examination, and was awarded a merit scholarship.

In Bihar, at the time, there were two main currents of political feeling. Bihar was the first place in the country where a terrorist bomb was exploded. The first political robbery also took place in Bihar. The bomb was set off by Khudiram Bose in Muzzaffarpur. The robbery took place in Shahabad, organised by Arjun Lal Sethi. The other current was Gandhian. At Champaran, Gandhi had already won a great victory against the English indigo planters, through *satyagraha*.

The violent method versus the non-violent one. Jayaprakash was faced with a crucial decision. But before he decided, he wanted to familiarise himself with the arguments, for and against.

He started by reading Gandhi's writings. He read the *Gita*, and about Gandhi's life. He discarded his fashionable clothes and donned khadi. Instead of shirt and coat, he wore a khadi kurta, He took off his English style shoes. It was not easy. Khadi did not look as nice as the clothes made from fine English yarn. It made one look like a villager. But that was what most of the people in the country were and still are— the real India.

On the other hand, Jayaprakash was also attracted to the extremist position. He recalls a strange incident. Very early one morning, there was commotion at Sarasvati Bhavan. Nearby, the famous historian, Professor Jadunath Sarkar, was staying, The police surrounded his house, and then searched it. Inside, a young member of the Revolutionary Party was hiding. Revolutionary Party ! Jayaprakash's interest grew. There was an underground cell of revolutionaries in Patna. Most of its members were Bengalis. To Jayaprakash here was a potent brew of valour and romance.

One day, he heard a shout: 'Kill the whites: stuff them into gunny bags !' (*Goran ko maar-maar boran men bharihon.*)

The revolutionaries met near the river, sometimes in dilapidated buildings. They had bombs and weapons. One of them said, 'Bengal is ready. Punjab is ready. Maharashtra is almost ready. Why is Bihar lagging behind ?'

A second man said, 'All government offices will be captured.'

A third: 'We will kill all the white men in Patna.'

'Come on, join us. Sign your name with the Revolutionary Army, Jayaprakash !'

Jayaprakash had heard about the moderates and extremists. But what was this Revolutionary Party ? By nature he was a soft-hearted boy. Gokhale was one of his idols. Benipuri records that Jayaprakash wrote a tearful poem when Gokhale died. Gokhale was a first influence on J.P. Then Gandhi, with his simplicity, his identification with the common man had a profound impact on him. And then this new temptation. But before he could make contact with the revolutionaries, they had gone into hiding. The Chief of Police from Calcutta, a man named Jackson, had come to Patna with a huge force. At this the revolutiouaries waded the river and crossed over to the other side.

Sitting by himself on the steps leading down to the Ganga, in front of Patna College, deep in thought . . . . How did this nation become enslaved ? Why has it not made any progress ? There is no shortage of great men—*rishis* and writers—so why are we lagging behind ? This a scientific age. It is science that has put the European nations where they are. India needs scientists.

The boy decides, 'I will become a scientist.'

When he joins Patna College, he opts for Science.

On his table, there is a unique assortment of books. On the one hand, Hindi newspapers, newsletters, *Bharat Bharati, Priyapravas, Ramcharitamanas*. On the other, physics, chemistry and mathematics books.

He had never heard Shambhu Babu talk forcefully. But one day, he heard him shouting: 'How is this possible ? He doesn't listen to his family ? He is violating his *dharma-karma.*'

'What is the matter, Shambhuji ?'

'Oho, Baulji ! I was just saying . . . .'

'Why were you talking so loudly ?'

'Oh, I was a little excited.'

Jayaprakash smiled slowly. Shambhu Babu then said, 'Baulji, come with me to Rajendra Babu's place. Braj Kishor Babu will be there.'

'What ?'

'Braj Kishor Babu !'

Braj Kishor Babu—the man who was Bihar Congress Chief from 1921 to 1923. The man who was responsible for calling Gandhi to Champaran. Also, the representative of the first Bihar Government to the Imperial Council. The man who was the greatest single influence on Rajendra Prasad when he was still a student.

At that time, the Sadaqat Ashram had not been built. Rajendra Babu had come to Patna from Calcutta, and was practising at the High Court. He was staying in a building very near the offices of the *Searchlight.*

Braj Kishor Babu was pleased to see Baulji. He felt this was the kind of man he wanted Prabha, his daughter, to marry. Harsood Pal and Phoolrani were told about the proposal. Jayaprakash was eighteen years old. They were married in June 1919 in a grand style.

Matrimony pushed Jayaprakash in a decisive direction. His immediate political choice was made. For one, it was a matrimonial alliance with one of the biggest political figures in Bihar. Further, Prabha's younger sister, Vidyavati, married Rajendra Babu's eldest son, Mrityunjay. With the matrimonial alliance the political connection grew taut.

Prabhavati was a favourite of her father's. He had brought her up exactly as though she were a boy. She wore male garments—dhoti, kurta, pyjama—before she was married. She had not been sent to school, but was given a thorough education at home. Her mother would want her to wear jewellery and fine clothes, but she was not fond of them. Ultimately, her grandmother, mother and father insisted that she must wear them for her wedding. Prabha said, 'I was a very active child. If I saw any kind of work in progress, I would want to join in. If the gardener was working in the garden, I felt I should be working with him. If Babaji (the cook) was in the kitchen, then I would be there too. I would insist on making the food, and if he protested, I would threaten to put out the fire. I wanted to do all the work with my own hands. It was only when I got married that I understood that I should start wearing jewellery. And I wore fine clothes.'

As Jayaprakash approached manhood, the political situation in the country ways simmering. There was no way by which Jayaprakash could have remained unaffected by the excitement and turmoil.

It was the second year of his marriage. His Intermediate examination was only twenty days away. Gandhiji had begun his Non-cooperation movement. Maulana Abul Kalam Azad had come to Patna. His great eloquence moved thousands of young men to join the freedom struggle. Jayaprakash recalls that period, 'I remember one January morning in 1921, when I attended a mass meeting at Patna and had the opportunity to listen to one of the foremost leaders of the Non-cooperation movement. He was not a very old man, but his words were like magic. I was completely overwhelmed. As it happened, there was another meeting taking place next to the one I was attending. We discovered that it was being addressed by Pandit Motilal Nehru's son. In those days, there were no loud-speakers, and large meetings were broken up into more manage-able groups and addressed by different speakers. The man's enthusiasm electrified the audience. That was why he was later called the "father of words". The next morning, we saw a strange sight. Students of the Patna colleges marched in a procession to Rajendra Babu's house to offer themselves for the cause. Seeing the students, Rajendra Babu was left speech-less, and tears poured down his cheeks.'

Jayaprakash was racked by doubt. But ultimately, he decided to give up his college carreer.

Although Gandhiji's Non-cooperation plans had been accept-ed by a Special Session of the Congress at Calcutta, the leader-ship had not yet agreed about whether students should be urged to give up their schools and colleges. This matter was finally cleared up at the Nagpur session, where Non-coopera-tion in all its aspects was accepted. Not only students, but people from all walks of life were asked to non-cooperate with the British Government. J.P. remembers that it was December of 1920 when Gandhiji came to Patna: 'I saw him for the first time. There was a huge crowd at the park, and I was one of that huge swell of people. All the Non-cooperators from college and other institutions were there. Rajendra Babu and Manoranjan Babu were also there. Manoranjan Babu sang an English song in Bhojpuri.'

This was the famous meeting at which several lawyers and government servants gave in their resignation letters. Deshbandhu Chittaranjan Das and Motilal Nehru had given up their careers at the Bar. In Patna, Maulana Majharul Haq and Rajendra Babu did likewise.

Jayaprakash's decision to abandon his studies was naturally a shock for his family. His middle-aged father saw this as somewhat a rash thing to do. But he did not try to stop Jayaprakash from doing what he thought was right.

And so, like thousands of other men, Jayaprakash responded to the call for Non-cooperation and left college. Some of the brightest students from Patna College also gave up their studies. Among them were Singheshvar, Krishna Ballabh Sahay, Pushkar Thakur, Phoolanprasad Varma and Vishveshvar Dayal—all of them played an important role in Bihar's politics in later years.

Jayaprakash did not become a Non-cooperator because of Gandhi's moral and spiritual charisma. He was motivated primarily by patriotism and the determination to win freedom was the sole factor in his decision to become a Non-cooperator.

In 1922, events took a strange turn. In February, the massacre took place at Chauri Chaura, and Gandhi called off Non-cooperation. Jayaprakash was forced to reassess the whole situation.

The next day, he went to the Bihar Vidyapeeth. This was an institution which the leaders of the nationalist movement had started for all those who had become Non-cooperators and left government colleges. Jayaprakash went on to do his Intermediate (Science) examination from here, and passed with honours. But the Vidyapeeth had no facilities for further studies in science. So he went to Professor Phooldev Sahay Varma, and was privately tutored. The opportunity of going on to the Benares Hindu University for further studies offered itself, but Jayaprakash would not consider joining an institution funded by the British Government. As it happened, he had read some books about America at Swami Satyadev's house, and had also heard him talk about the place. He made up his mind to go there and continue his academic career.

J.P.'s father was very reluctant to allow him to go so far away. His mother burst into tears at the thought. Even Braj Kishor Babu, who had encouraged and helped so many students to go abroad, was against the idea. Shambhu Babu was unhelpful too.

Soon after, a young man named Bholadutt Pant came to Braj Kishor Babu to ask for help in getting to America. Bholadutt was a Garhwali boy, a student at the Benares Hindu University. Jayaprakash met him at Braj Kishor's house, and the two became good friends. Jayaprakash decided to go to America with Bholadutt. Immediately after, he went to Calcutta and had his passport made. But there was disappointing news. The newspapers carried articles about Indian students in America, saying that they were finding life very hard with rising prices and scarce jobs. For the time being, Jayaprakash decided to stay back. Bholadutt Pant continued on his way alone, but wrote back to say that the news items were completely baseless. He told Jayaprakash to come along, and also bring his wife along. Jayaprakash showed the letter to Prabhavati, and she helped to strengthen his resolve.

Jayaprakash then made another trip to Calcutta and made all the arrangements for the voyage. He sent word to his family that on a particular date, he would be sailing for America. There was great consternation at home. Prabhavati, at the time, was visiting her parents. Braj Kishor Babu asked her, 'Beti, did you know about this ?'

"Yes."

'Oho, so you said goodbye and came home !'

Jayaprakash was then 20 years old. Before he left, he wanted to see his wife. He arrived at Srinagar, at his in-laws' house.

'I am leaving. I will be back soon.'

Prabhavati looked at him tearfully. He said, 'Why don't you also study, for as long as I am away ?'

'Can I go to the Sabarmati ashram ?'

'Do whatever you really want to do.'

Jayaprakash left for the United Satates of America and Prabhavati went to Sabarmati. One of them moved toward socialism, the other towards philosophical Gandhism.

About his mother's reaction, Jayaprakash recalls, 'My mother cried and said, "You have been married so recently, and now, who knows when you will return ?" She didn't believe that I would come back at all. She thought I might get married again in America. We were living at a place called Nasrigunj, in Shahabad, where my father was *ziladar*. When it was time to go, I touched my mother's feet and got into the *ekka*. My father came out to see me off, but I could hear my mother wailing loudly from within the house. It must have been heart-rending for her. . . .'

August 16, 1922. Calcutta city. Time: evening. The same river Ganga, but called the Hooghly here. A cargo boat on this river; it's name, *Janus*. Tonight, it will sail for Japan. On top, on the second class deck, stands Jayaprakash. The steamer pulls out. Holding the railing, he watches the shoreline receding. When there is nothing more to be seen, he goes into his cabin. And all the pent-up emotion of the past few weeks wells up inside him.

On the voyage, Jayaprakash met two other students. Both of them were from Hyderabad State—Sitaram Gopal Reddy and Harishchandra Ramarao Pradhan. In the Bay of Bengal, the voyage became rough, and both these boys wanted to return. Jayaprakash dissuaded them from this foolishness.

From Rangoon, the ship steamed towards Malaya. Two centuries earlier, hundreds of coolies from Bihar and Uttar Pradesh had been sent here . . . .From Rangoon to Penang. Then on to Singapore. In those days, the British used Singapore as a major naval base. Hong Kong to Japan—and on the way, a great typhoon. The ship reached Kobe a full thirty days after it left Hong Kong. Jayaprakash liked Japan a lot. Particularly the small, clean houses, the flowering shrubs in the courtyards. From Kobe, Jayaprakash visited Osaka, where he met Mahadevlal Sarraf. It turned out that Mahadevlal was also on his way to America, but had stayed on in Japan to earn some money by proof-reading for a newspaper called *Manichi*. From Osaka he went to Yokohama by train, where he was to catch the ship that would take him to America. The ship was called *Teyomaru*, (the Sun-ship). Ten days later, it steamed out of the harbour.

Jayaprakash reached California on the eighth of October, 1922. He had very little money. It would take a while before he could start studying again. America had been hit by a massive inflation in the aftermath of the first world war. Jayaprakash was, moreover, completely on his own.

In California, there was a small settlement of Indian immigrants, mostly Sikhs and Pathans. From them, he found out about the University of California, Berkeley. The Indian students already at the university had formed a society called the Nalanda Club. The Nalanda in Bihar ? Jayaprakash went to the Nalanda Club, and was given a place to stay. He shared a room with Dr. K.V. Menon, who was in his fourth year of study.

It was October. Three more months before the university opened. Jayaprakash decided to earn some money in the meantime. The Y.M.C.A. ran an employment bureau for students of the university looking for jobs. But they were unhelpful. J.P. then heard that Indian foremen recruited labour in a nearby village named Maryville. He was told that in every gang they accepted a few Indian workers. With Reddy, Jayaprakash went to Maryville. He was surprised at the "Indian-ness" of the immigrant workers. They asked eagerly for news about the Independence struggle of India and about Gandhi.

One of the foremen, a Pathan named Sher Khan, took a liking to the two boys, and recruited them into his gang. Sher Khan was a foreman of a gang of grape-pickers who worked on acres of vineyards that belonged to Mr. C.B. Harter. Harter also owned orchards of almonds, peaches and pears.

They had to work a nine-hour day, with an hour's break for lunch. The wage was orty cents an hour, about four dollars a day. At the time, that was equivalent to about fourteen rupees.

Jayaprakash worked ten hours a day, seven days a week. He did not take Sundays or holidays off. He netted eighty dollars a fortnight. He got on very well with Sher Khan, whose kindness taught Jayaprakash an early lesson in respect for another man's religion. As long as he was working with the gang, Sher Khan did not allow beef to be cooked in the camp.

By the end of November, Jayaprakash had earned enough to support himself at the university for a while. Soon after, he was given admission to the second year of the university programme.

Jayaprakash was very impressed with the California University. Twenty thousand students, miles and miles of beautiful campus. There were more girls than boys, and they studied, played and lived together without any segregation between the sexes. Jayaprakash was also very impressed with the laboratories, and the general facilities for serious work. The Professors were very eminent, and sustained a relaxed, easy relationship with the students.

At the end of the first semester, Jayaprakash got an "A" in his written papers, though he did not fare as well in his Practicals. But he had run out of money. Tuition fees had gone up to one hundred and fifty dollars a semester. What was he to do ? Jayaprakash contacted his friend Bholadutt Pant. Bholadutt was studying at the University of Iowa, where the eminent Indian scientist, Dr. Sudhindra Bose was a Professor. From Bholadutt, Jayaprakash learnt that the fees at Iowa were much lower than at California, and he decided to migrate there.

Before leaving, he had to earn some money, so he went back to Maryville. He was accepted into a predominantly Sikh gang, but he did not like the atmosphere and left. He then found a job packing fruit crates, and after earning enough money, proceeded to Iowa.

He stayed with Bholadutt for two semesters, a full year. With four or five other students, they took turns at cooking for themselves. From time to time, Jayaprakash supplemented his meagre resources by polishing furniture. In the winter, he shovelled snow off the driveways of affluent homes. Working off and on, he managed to earn enough to support himself.

It was in America that Jayaprakash became "J.P." His Professors found it easier this way; and the appellation stuck.

At Iowa, J.P. studied under Professor Albert Weiss. One

of his subjects was Chemical Engineering for which he needed
a certain aptitude for drawing. With a little smile, J.P. recalls
that this was one department in which he was woefully weak,
and he failed in draughtsmanship. But in all other respects
he was a brilliant student.

After Iowa, J.P. went to Chicago, where he stayed for two
and a half years. In Chicago, once again, he worked at a
number of jobs. For a short while he even worked in a meat
factory, but he was so revolted by the sight of rows of car-
casses, that he was put to work in the power-house.
'Although, by that time I had become a nonvegetarian, I
could not stomach the sight of meat for many weeks after that
. . . I learned to play tennis there.'

And, 'I didn't only clean toilets, I also worked as a
shoeshine boy. Something of Gandhiji's values had rubbed
off on me. Part of my willingness, however, was due to the
way we lived at home. My parents were always very kind to
poor people, to people of a lower station in life. Although
our family owned land, that did not bring them much income.
We earned according to the amount we worked.'

In America, J.P. began to read European literature. In
particular, Anatole France, Ibsen and Gorky. As economic
conditions worsened, however, J.P. found that he has to do
things against his inclination in order to survive. Like other
Indian students, he hawked ersatz scent, creams and hair
lotions "made from choice Himalayan herbs," that promised
the impossible ! 'These herbs make dark skins fair, kinky hair
straight !" A chemistry student in his senior year had stooped
to this ?

One day a strange thing happened. A young girl bought
a whole lot of the magical potions from J.P., and asked him
to call at the house for payment. When he went to the apart-
ment, she invited him in and offered him a cup of coffee. But
When J.P. asked for the money, she said 'Money ? Is it just
money you want ?' and made her amorous intentions quite
clear . . . J.P. had to depart in a hurry.

Thd State of Wisconsin was regarded, at the time, as one
of the most progressive States in the American Union. It had
a good university and two of its Presidents were reputed to

be socialists. This was where J.P. went next.

Again, J.P. had to spend his vacations earning his keep—
he washed dishes and served food in a restaurant, polished
floors, and worked in boiler-rooms, coaling booths, barber
shops, etc. But at least they were more self-respecting than
selling ersatz potions.

Here, at Wisconsin, J.P. made a lot of friends—not only
Americans, but Russians, Poles, Germans, Dutchmen and the
French also. One of his closest friends, a Polish Jew named
Abraham Landy, taught and studied at the university. Landy
was a member of the Bolshevik Party, and also, a member
of an underground communist cell at the university. J.P.
attended occasional meetings of this cell, and gradually identified with its ideological line.

It was during this time that he read two books by the noted
Indian communist, M.N. Roy. They were *The Aftermath of Non-
cooperation* and *India in Transition.* Roy was living in the USSR
at the time, as an honoured official of the Comintern, and
edited a journal called *New Message.* J.P. was greatly influenced
by the articles in *New Message,* and took a new interest in
the activities of the American Communist Party, which was
led by the famous Mexican Marxist, Manuel Gomez.

J.P. said to me, 'I am talking about 1924, before Lenin died.
Later during the same year, Lenin was succeeded by Stalin.
I read Lenin's and Trotsky's writings avidly. I was convinced
that what they were doing was right. But this conviction led
me to question the value of studying Science. The immediate
task was to win freedom for our country. Why not familiarise
myself with the social science ? So I switched courses, and
for my graduation, chose sociology as my major subject, and
economics as a subsidiary.'

It was a big step for him. It was not as though he had
chosen Science because it had no relevance to the country.
In fact, he had reasoned specifically that a backward nation
needed scientists to pull itself up to the level of the developed
countries. But now he argued differently. Unless the whole
basis of society was changed, science would serve no useful
function. A small handful of capitalists would stand to gain.

But now he had to face the next question—how did one go

about changing society ?

Wisconsin counted among its alumni two eminent social scientists. One was Professor Edward Ross , the other, Professor Young. Ross, was regarded as the doyen of American social scientists. Young's forte was social psychiatry.

At the urging of Landy and Gomez, however, J.P. was persuaded that the best way to familiarise himself with socialist theory was to go to Russia. So J.P. quit Wisconsin, though he decided first to go to Chicago to earn some money.

It was the winter of 1926, and the Depression was setting in. J.P. recalls, 'There were no jobs. I would leave the house early in the morning after a cup of coffee. But wherever I went, there were signs that said "No help wanted", "No Asiatics wated", "No coloured people". . .'

The poor diet and the exposure to wind and cold, as he searched for a job, affected his health. It started as a mild cough, developed into acute tonsillitis and then assumed dangerous proportions. For a full year he laboured under illness. He lost his voice, his body grew thin and weak. J.P. still shudders when he recalls those days. But help was at hand. 'My friend Chandra Singh and his wife looked after me like a father and mother. Those two friends, Reddy and Pradhan, and many altogether new acquaintances were a great help !'

After a long while, J.P. was forced to write home. He told his parents that he had been ill, and had recovered, but had to borrow some money. Could they send him some money to repay his debts ?

Harsood Pal mortgaged his land and sent some money promptly. But he found out that J.P. wanted to go to Russia, and he wrote him a letter asking him to come home instead. Braj Kishor and Rajendra Babu also wrote letters urging him not to stay away any longer. 'Do not go to Russia,' Rajendra Babu wrote. 'Come back to India. If you insist on going, then you can make arrangements to go from here. We will help you.' And so, his plans of going to Russia were dropped.

J.P. went back to Wisconsin to continue with the social sciences programme. But before the term was out, Landy moved to the University of Ohio. J.P. followed him there, and remained at Ohio for the rest of his stay in America.

Here, J.P. had the opportunity of studying under Professor Miller, whose researches in developmental economics had hit the world like a bombshell. J.P. completed his B.A. and was awarded a scholarship of thirty dollars. And then after a single term of his Master's programme, he was appointed an Assistant Professor. Now he was completely free of the need to do odd jobs to keep himself in pocket. He studied for his M.A. in Social Science, and taught some of the junior classes. He was earning eighty dollars a month.

In April 1929, J.P. received a letter from his wife from the Sabarmati *ashram* telling him about her vow of observing *brahmacharya*. What had inspired her was this: the second time that Prabhavati went to the Sabarmati *ashram*, she had been impressed by the fact that all the inmates had renounced something dear to them. They lived celibate lives. Prabhavati felt that she too had to renounce something. She went to Gandhiji and talked to him about the matter. At first, he was not enthusiastic, but she persisted; and at length he said, 'Alright, you are married, but you should discuss the matter with your husband first.'

Prabhavati wrote to J.P. and told him how she felt about it. J.P. had said earlier, that if they wanted to serve the country, they had to sacrifice their family life, and the luxury of having children. In his reply, J.P. said that he was agreeable. When they met again after his return, they would discuss the matter. What could he say in a letter ?

The full import of Prabhavati's decision did not strike J.P. until Gandhiji wrote and said, 'If you want to marry again, you may do so.' J.P. wrote back, 'You are free to make your own decision. I will accept it.'

Prabhavati made her first entry in her diary on the day she received this letter : 'April, 1929. I woke up at four o'clock. Brushed my teeth; prayer, personal work, bath and breakfast. I walked a little with Bapu. Then prepared the water for his bath, cooked the food, ate. Rubbed some oil on Bapu's feet. Slept. Fanned Bapu. Cleaned up. Then sat a while with Bapu. Bapu asked me to translate a Gujarati letter into Hindi, which I did. Read *Navjivan*. Read the *Gita* and some English.

Wrote down some *shlokas* from the *Gita*. Tidied up the office. Repaired the *charkha*. Soaked the yarn. Read the mail. Wrote a letter to America. Went walking with Bapu. Cooked the food. Prayed. Massaged Bapu's feet. Made entries in my diaries. Went to sleep at 10 o'clock.'

J.P. did his Master's degree at Wisconsin. His thesis topic was, "Social Variation". The thesis, which was praised, had been written under the supervision of Professor N.B. Dumley.

What is society ? How is it formed ? How does it change ? What are the forces of change ? What are the laws of transition ? These were some of the questions with which his thesis was concerned. Darwin, in his treatise on evolution, had argued for natural selection—that only the fittest survive, others perish. The principle of natural selection had been applied to society by Professor Keller of Yale University. J.P.'s thesis extended and refined Keller's analysis of social change.

Professor Dumley was very pleased with J.P. In his letter of recommendation (May 3, 1929), he said ;

. . . Intellectually, it seems to me, Mr. Narayan ranks as high or higher than any student I have ever had. He is a careful and critical thinker, and a searcher after truth, and of course, he is a wide reader. He is, in every sense, a scholar in the making . . . . I would strongly recommend him because of his intellectual power and his interest in human welfare, not as a prepared leader, but as having the germs of leadership. He is aggressive in thought but not in action. . . .

J.P.'s student days in America were a great learning experience. He had worked at an odd assortment of jobs; he had studied at a number of universities, and he had mixed his academic interests, so that he emerged as an extraordinarily mature and well-rounded individual. But more surprising was the fact that he also found time to enjoy himself. The cinema was one passion. J.P. told me, 'Those were the days of Mary Pickford. She was at the top, and very famous. Before I left, in 1929, Greta Garbo had started appearing on screen. I saw a lot of films. At one time, I began to learn how to dance at the Recreation Room. I didn't have enough time, and never became any good. I didn't have an ear for music. You cannot dance if you cannot keep time. My friends would be there and girls from the university. But eventually, I learnt nothing.'

It was a poor existence. Work and study, for most of his university career, proceeded side by side, and taxed his health. There was never really enough money for him to take it easy. He had to borrow clothes for the dance lessons ! He pressed his clothes by folding them under the mattress of his bed. And as his serious interests increased, the time which he might have given to recreation was completely taken up. Being a communist and working for the labour movement were time-consuming activities.

'I became great friends with Miller, my Professor. At Wisconsin there was a girl called Miss Anthony Baker who was not in my year, but we worked together. We became very good friends.'

Mathematics was J.P.'s forte. Apart from higher calculus, he specialised in mathematical probability and trade forecasting. Even when he switched his interest from science to the humanities, his interest in mathematics did not wane. He also devoted long hours of study to bacteriology, which was a new subject at the time. His other interests were economics, psychology, history, literature, anatomy and kinship. Linguistics was another area of knowledge to which J.P. devoted a lot of his attention.

No other Indian leader approached the field of politics with so much learning, so many varied disciplines of thought behind him. It is a measure of his humility that he has kept the evidence of this awesome learning from some of his closest associates. J.P. had behind him, not only formal learning, but experience culled from working at jobs as widely different as cleaning toilets and teaching at university as well. It is an impressive record, but looking at J.P. and listening to him talk about America, one would think he led a humdrum, ordinary life when he was there as a student.

All of his professors were struck by his independence of thought, and impressed with the clarity and brilliance of his mind. The Professor of Economics at Ohio University, Professor A.B. Wolfe wrote (May 1, 1929) :

Mr. Narayan held a university scholarship in sociology here. I have come into contact with him in courses in the

history of economic thought and the economics of population. I have found him—as I am sure others here have also
—a young man of more than ordinary independence and
maturity of thought. He shows distinctly an enquiring turn
of mind and a critical capacity, rare even in the better class
of graduate students. He is a fine-appearing man, a thorough
gentleman and in my opinion, a thorough student. I have
noted that he always has an interest in the larger and deeper
problems of economics, rather than in matters of technical
detail. . . .

Prof. Charles A. Dice wrote (May 2, 1929):

I have known Mr. J.P. Narayan, one of our graduate
students from India, quite closely since last September
both as a student in my classes and as a man among other
graduate students. His work with me is consistently 'A'
grade. He is open-minded, eager to make intellectual contacts
and has plenty of originality. In short, Mr. Narayan belongs
to the highest class of graduate ability. . . .

Prof. Miller was of the opinion (May 7, 1929) :

Mr. J.P. Narayan is a fine candidate for a Moral Leadership Fellowship. He is one of the ablest students I have ever
had, both keen and deep. His whole outlook is based on a
desire to know how to do something to help society. He is
well balanced and does not let his desires interfere with his
objectives. . . .

After completing his M.A., Jayaprakash started making
arrangements to do his Ph.D. But before any of these plans
could take shape, he received a letter from his father, telling
him that his mother was seriously ill.

Jayaprakash decided to return. He left Ohio, but he did
not have enough money to pay the fare for the voyage back
to India, so he went to New York. His old friend, Reddy, was
there, and had set up a perfumery business. Bholadutt Pant
was in New York too. Jayaprakash started working in hotels
and factories to earn some money. New York strengthened an
emergent attitude in him. His experience of working in the
glittering, hotels of the great city gave him an abiding distaste
for capitalist civilisation.

One evening, Jayaprakash was standing at the balustrade,

gazing out at the ships in harbour, worrying about his mother.
A voice behind him said, 'Hallo, J.P !'

Looking back, J.P. found a smiling Aurangabadkar, who
said, 'I had hoped we could go back to India together. We
could have taken my car, and motored through Europe before
we reached India.'

He put his hand on J.P.'s shoulder, and said, 'Tell me, will
you leave tomorrow with me for India ?'

'I would like to, but not just yet. In a few days.'

'You mean you are collecting money for your fare ?'

J.P. did not reply.

Aurangabadkar thumped him on the back and said, 'We
must leave tomorrow. I will pay your fare up to England.'

Then followed a tearful, sentimental, farewell to friends,
colleagues and professors. He had to leave behind him seven
years of association. He had come here as a lad of twenty in
October, 1922. Now, in September, 1929, he was leaving as a
mature and highly developed man.

The ship sailed for England. Aurangabadkar journeyed on
to India, but J.P. had to write home to his father to ask for
some money.

It took twenty-eight days for the money to arrive. In the
interval, he explored London and its surrounds. At Oxford, he
met Radhakrishnan, who was Professor of Indian Philosophy
at the time. He was engaged in trying to form a society for
peace and international amity after the ravages of the first
world war. J.P. had a long discussion with him about the
Bolshevik Party.

With the money from home, J.P. bought a third class ticket
on an Australian liner. The ship halted at France, then at
Naples, Port Said, the Suez Canal and then sailed straight to
Colombo. J.P. disembarked at Colombo, and caught a train
to Dhanushkodi. . . . from there to Madras, and then on to
Calcutta and Patna, and then to Sitab Diyara to rejoin his
parents.

Chapter Three

AT the time that J.P. returned from America, nationalist feeling had reached a peak of frenzy. Early in 1930, Gandhi launched the Salt *satyagraha*. J.P. joined the fray with whole-hearted enthusiasm.

I questioned him about this period of his life. He told me : 'I returned to Patna. Prabhavati was with Bapu. I went straight to the house of my brother-in-law. Didi (J.P.'s sister) was not there either. I took off my Western style clothes and put on a dhoti-kurta, and left for our village. People wondered how I would adjust to conditions in the village after so many years abroad. My mother was cooking over a wood fire, and was a little embarrassed that I might see her working in such primitive condition. But soon, I had surprised people with my reversion to a village style of life.'

This was the 23rd of November, 1929.

'What happened then ?'

'Oh, I don't remember all the details. I went to Prabha's village, Srinagar. There, I met Ishvar Babu, Rajendra Babu and Mrityunjay Babu. Vidyavati, my sister-in-law was there too.'

A significant incident may be related here. When J.P., the Marxist and atheist, first set foot in his home, he had to undergo *shuddhipuja* or purification rites. Why had he submitted to a ritual which he did not believe in ? I asked him this question.

'It had something to do with the kind of person I was.

I was not fanatical about my beliefs. By temperament, I had firm beliefs, but while holding on to them, I was willing to look at the other side of the picture, and make adjustments. I was a Marxist and therefore, an atheist, and perhaps that kind of person should not undergo *shuddhi*. But my father and mother, the rest of the family, they were not non-believers like me. They were all religious people. They were very glad to see me again after all those years, and it did not seem the right thing to do to announce that I did not believe. It would have shattered them . . .'

A few days after Jayaprakash's return, a session of the Bihar Provincial Congress was held at Monghyr. Rajendra Prasad presided over the meetings, and Sardar Patel was there too. The victory at Bardoli had raised their spirits and given the session an added importance. The chief issue at the Monghyr session was whether the nationalist movement should demand full independence, or whether a promise of dominion status was enough. In those days, this was the big question. The Congressmen were all for the more radical demand, complete independence. The older leaders opposed them. Men like Swami Sahajanand Saraswati and Prajapati Mishra lent the weight of their authority to the more moderate party. But even then, when the votes were totted up, the younger section prevailed. J.P. was at that session as an observer.

From Sitab Diyara, J.P. went with Prabhavati to Wardha to meet Bapu. Prabha went because she wanted to return to her duties at the *ashram*. J.P. went because he wanted to meet Gandhiji. It was the second week of December, 1929. They arrived at Wardha, and were welcomed with open arms by Ba and Bapu. Ba spared nothing to make J.P. feel as a member of the family.

As soon as she arrived at the *ashram*, Prabhavati slipped into the life she was used to. The next day, Bapu said to her, 'Who is looking after Jayaprakash's needs ?'

'I do not know,' Prabha replied.

'Look, *beti*, you are married to him. It is your *dharma* to minister to his needs.'

Prabhavati accepted what Bapu told her. From then on, she washed J.P.'s clothes, cooked for him, did all his work.

J.P. recalls: 'Before the Congress was to meet in Lahore, the Working Committee was scheduled to meet at Wardha, where Bapu was staying. I was prevailed upon to stay at Wardha for the meeting. I was treated with a lot of respect because of Prabha's standing at the *ashram*.'

After the Working Committee deliberations, Jayaprakash and Jawaharlal Nehru were introduced to each other.

'I liked Jawaharlal and he liked me. We talked a little. Not too much. Then we went upstairs to talk to Bapu. I cannot recall what Bapu said to us,' J.P. said.

During those days, an Englishman named Reginald Reynolds was staying at the *ashram*, the same man who carried Gandhiji's views back to London after the meeting was over. One day, he came upon J.P. reading a book, sitting outside the *ashram*.

'What are you reading?' Reynolds asked.

'*Sceptical Essays*.'

'You sit outside Gandhiji's *ashram* and read a book with a title like that ?' he said with a twinkle in his eye.

From Wardha, J.P. and Prabha accompanied Gandhiji to Lahore. Jawaharlal presided over the Congress session. Thousands of people marched in tumultuous processions. Great shouts of *Inquilab Zindabad* ! (Long live the Revolution !) rent the air. This was the session at which Nehru announced that Congress would fight for complete Independence (*poorna swaraj*).

J.P. and Prabha stayed with Brajkishanji Chandiwala in Lahore. Every morning, before dawn, Prabha would get up and pray. J.P. was never awake for these religious sessions.

The meetings were drawing to a close. The big question was: what will Prabha do now ? Would she go with Bapu to Wardha or choose to stay with her husband ? Neither husband nor wife seemed to want to broach this ticklish subject. They had not yet discussed the issue of Prabha's *brahmacharya*. J.P.'s friends, particularly his communist and socialist friends taunted him for allowing Prabha to stay with Gandhiji. 'That is what he does to women,' they told him. 'Do not let her stay at the *ashram*.' At length, J.P. accosted Prabha, 'Will you come with me ?'

She replied, 'Yes, I will come. But I promised that I would go back for a short while.'

'No, you must come with me.'

Prabha went to look for Bapu to seek his advice, and found him engrossed in a meeting. She told him what had happened. Bapu said, 'It is your *dharma*, your duty. You must go with Jayaprakash.'

She bent down to touch Bapu's feet, and burst into tears. Bapu comforted her, but was firm in his advice: 'No, you must go and live with your husband. Try and understand each other. You must leave the *ashram*. For you, your husband is more important.'

One day, Jawaharlal came up to J.P. and asked him what he intended doing. Jayaprakash answered that he wanted to work for the country and join the Congress.

'In that case, come to Allahabad,' said Jawaharlal.

As Congress President, Jawaharlal wanted to appoint Jayaprakash a Secretary in the Labour Department of the Congress. Mirza Bakur Ali was tipped for the post, but for some reason he did not show up at Allahabad. Jayaprakash agreed to come to Allahabad and 'join'.

It was the beginning of 1930. Jayaprakash was in Allahabad, and Prabha with him. They rented a house in the Georgetown locality for sixty rupees a month—another fourteen rupees paid for the furniture. Their total income was a hundred and fifty rupees a month.

One day, Jawaharlal visited them, 'Where did you get this furniture from ?' Then he laughed and said, 'If you live in this fashion, how will you manage on a hundred and fifty rupees a month ?'

Nehru further said, 'Why are you unnecessarily spending so much money on the rent ? Why don't you come and stay at Swaraj Bhavan ?'

So that was where J.P. and Prabha moved next.

From this point onwards, the friendship between Jawaharlal Nehru and Jayaprakash deepened. Nehru became more and more impressed with J.P.'s acute intelligence. In fact, he was so pleased with J.P. that he wanted to appoint him to the post of permanent Minister which Raja Rao had just vacated.

J.P. was nominated soon after.

Soon after, the movement of 1930 began. But at about the same time, his mother fell ill, and J.P. returned to his home. His mother died at the end of this illness, and J.P. was unable to involve himself with the movement any more. He stayed on in the village for a while. Financially, the family was in dire straits, and J.P. had no thought of leaving them to fend for themselves.

About this time Kamala Nehru wrote Prabha a letter ;

Dear Prabha,

Jayaprakashji should come back and attend to his work. To stop his work for the country because his mother has died does not seem right. His mother would be distressed to know that he has forsaken a 'true' mother (his country) and is wallowing in sadness.

Kamala

The Congress celebrated 'Independence Day' all over India on 26th January, 1930. Gandhi, authorised by the Congress, commenced the civil disobedience movement in March by starting the Salt *satyagraha* and the march to Dandi. He declared : 'At present Indian self-respect is symbolised in a handful of salt in the *satyagrahi's* hand. Let the fist be broken but let there be no surrender of the salt.' The whole country was inflamed.

The Independence movement swelled in Bihar. From his place in Sadaqat Ashram, Braj Kishor Babu directed the activities of uncoordinated wings of the movement in Bihar. The British Government unleashed a brutal campaign to quash the movement, but there was no evidence, in Bihar, of the movement losing its vigour. Braj Kishor Babu was arrested and sent to Hazaribagh Jail. Sadaqat Ashram remained the headquarters of the agitation, where Maulana Majharul Huq and Rajendra Babu were still free to lead the movement.

J.P. and Prabha were quickly drawn into the centre of the agitation, and went to Allahabad. Gandhi was detained in May that year and in the next five months over 60,000 Indians courted imprisonment for non-violently defying the Salt Law, and picketing liquor and foreign cloth shops.

The Congress was banned, but its meetings continued and

its public support grew, and leaflets and directives issued by
it continued to find their way to all parts of the country.

It was the first time in the history of British rule that the
Government was humbled. Lord Irwin summoned Gandhi
for talks in February 1931. The *satyagraha* was called off, the
ban on the Congress was lifted and it reassembled in a grand
conference at Karachi. Gandhi left for the Round Table
talks in London. The Viceroy agreed to release the civil disobedience prisoners, and to allow people living on the coast
to manufacture salt.

During this period, J.P. received news that his father had
had a paralytic stroke. There was no option for him but to take
leave of absence from his work. The family was in grave
financial trouble. His father had met J.P.'s requests for money
while he was abroad only by mortgaging his land and securing a loan. Now there was no money to take care of the
father's medical bill. Besides, the rest of the family had to be
supported and the loan repayed.

J.P. wrote to Gandhi and described his predicament. Bapu
replied to say that J.P.'s primary loyalty was undoubtedly
towards his father and family, and that he must rush to
their aid. He also wrote to G.D. Birla, asking him if he
could somehow help J.P., suggesting that a teaching post at
Pilani College would do fine. The Government, however,
would not have permitted a political firebrand like J.P. to
teach at Pilani, and so, Birla offered J.P. a job as his
secretary.

It was with Birla that J.P. defined his attitude towards the
Indian capitalist class. If the industrialists had one foot in the
Sabarmati *ashram*, they had another in the Viceregal lodge
or in Whitehall. J.P. stayed with Birla for six months until
the Gandhi-Irwin pact was signed. Immediately after, Jawaharlal summoned J.P. to return to work for the now legal
Congress.

When J.P. returned to Swaraj Bhavan, he busied himself
in laying the foundations of the Trade Union movement.
He was particularly keen that the Congress should develop a
strong orientation towards labour, and eventually coalesce
with the separate working-class parties that were springing up.

Soon after J.P. returned, Prof. Herbert Miller visited him at Allahabad. J.P. took him to Patna, the ruins of Nalanda and to Kashi. At Kashi, they met Acharya Narendra Dev. They visited the Vidyapeeth because it had emerged as one of the leading centres of nationalist sentiment.

Back at Allahabad, J.P. introduced his Professor to Jawaharlal. Sitting in the majestic high-ceilinged rooms of Anand Bhavan, Miller asked Nehru : 'Do you not feel uneasy, living in a place like this and talking about socialism ?'

Nehru replied: 'It helps the efficiency of our work.' And, they both started laughing.

Prof. Miller gave a few speeches, but the British Government looked askance at his sympathy for the nationalist cause, and he was asked to leave the country. Furthermore, when Miller returned to America he was forced to resign from the State University.

And what of Prabhavati during all this time ? Both Prabha and Kamala Nehru had involved themselves in the nationalist movement as staunch Gandhians. At Allahabad they marched in processions, attended political meetings, joined striking workers and stood in the picket-lines. More important, they were an example and inspiration to hundreds of other women who followed in their footsteps.

Gandhi's non-violent crusade accomplished two things at once : it succeeded in arousing nationalist feeling even in the sleepiest corners of the country. It also achieved something more profound : the movement enabled people to shake off centuries of servility, to think anew, to cast off repressive social customs. With the political revolution came a moral and social revolution. Kamala Nehru and Prabha were thus not merely political agitators. They were missionaries of a new sensibility and a new society.

Prabha's diary became almost a political chronicle, reflecting her new interest in the outside world:

3-8-1930 : *Allahabad*
Read the newspapers. Last evening, in Bombay, Malaviyaji, Vallabhbhai and others were arrested. At five o' clock, marched in a procession from the Chowk.

5-8-1930 : Allahabad

At 7.30, I went to the Congress office. From there, to the school to help organise the strike and picketing. Came home at 12.15. Went to Modern School at 1.30, where there was a lathi-charge by the police. Returned at 3.00. Spun cotton. Went to a meeting at 6.30.

1932 : In Jail

On 3-2-1932, at 7.30 in the evening, we were arrested during a meeting at Tandonji's house. We were tried on the 8th, and sent to 'B' class jail. (18th) I was transferred to Lucknow Central Jail. A sweeperess and two sentries accompanied me. (28th) Today, *mami* (aunt) came to see me. I expected her to be allowed inside, but she was not permitted to come beyond the outer gates. That saddened me. (13th March) I was told that Jayaprakashji would be coming to see me. Waited for him. Then Gyanvati told me he would come the next day. Went to sleep. Did not sleep well. (24th April) Mataji, Vidyavati and Jayaprakashji came to see me. Both my brothers were there too, but they were not allowed in. Jayaprakashji brought soap, oil, etc. (30th April) Had my weight taken—76 pounds.

19-9-1932 : Lucknow Jail

Today I learnt that Jayaprakashji has been sentenced to a year's rigorous imprisonment. Also had news from Bapu, who is to go on a fast from the 20th. I am very worried about him. I do not know what is going to happen. To-morrow, the entire country will go on fast for 24 hours, and there will be prayers. We too have decided to fast, and to pray at 12 o' clock. I am very worried. Last night, went to bed very quickly after prayer. Did not manage to get any sleep for a very long while. I keep thinking about Bapu. I think of every incident that occurred while I was with him at the *ashram*. Last year, while I was ill, he looked after me in the jail. But today, I cannot do anything to help him. I keep wishing that I had some way of taking all his worries off his shoulders. I do not understand what to do. Cried for a while. Then slept.

20-9-1932 : *Lucknow Jail*

Today we took this vow: all of us sisters in this jail would
dedicate ourselves to Mahatma Gandhi's sacred vow. We
vowed that we would dedicate our lives to the physical,
mental and spiritual uplift of those people who are called
'untouchables'. We vowed that we would strive, when we
left this jail, to opening the doors of opportunity to this
class of men and women. We pray to God that Mahatmaji's
sacrifice bears fruit and that under his guidance, India attains
its freedom.

The Second Round Table Conference held in London in late
1931 did not go off well. To decide their future course of action,
the Congress Working Committee was due to meet in Bombay.
Jawaharlal Nehru, travelling with Tasadduk Shervani, was on
his way to Bombay. J.P. was in the next bogey. There was
speculation about whether the Government would try and
arrest Jawaharlal.

Jawaharlal and Shervani were arrested enroute at Naini.
Jayaprakash proceeded to Bombay alone.

Willingdon had made elaborate arrangement to scuttle the
Congress session. A dozen ordinances had been drawn up in
readiness. The Congress was declared an illegal body and within
a week, all its principal leaders were installed behind bars.
The Congress offices were occupied by the police. The
Secretary of State, Sir Samuel Hoare, announced in Parliament—'Congress is dead.'

The elegant Taj Hotel in Bombay. Shrimati Sarojini Naidu,
one of the residents. After the arrests, much of the responsibility of keeping the Congress organisation alive rests on her.
Wearing traditional Parsi attire, J.P. arrives in her room and
hands over a thick file of Congress papers and correspondence
that he has been carrying with him.

From Bombay, J.P. returns to Allahabad, where he learns
of the arrest of Prabha and Kamala. Then back to Bombay,
where he organises a secret meeting of the All-India Congress
Committee. J.P. and Lalji Mehrotra preside. Then again, in
disguise, he tours extensively through the cities and small
mofussil towns of the country, dragging out young political

workers from their homes, persuading them not to lose heart, to continue with the work.

J.P. lost all faith in the usefulness of Indian industrialists during this campaign. They were not prepared to take any risks, they cowered in fear from the repressive tactics of the Government. But the national movement rolled on, unobstructed. Right under Willingdon's nose, the Congress delegates met and deliberated in Chandni Chowk in the capital city of Delhi. The wave of arrests continued and the savage repression too went on.

About this time, J.P. helped to organise a secret meeting of the Congress Working Committee at Benares, at the home of Shiv Prasad Gupta. Dr. Kitchlew, Rajendra Babu, Rajagopalachari, Kiranshankar Rai, Anne Sahib and Madan Mohan Malaviya attended and led the proceedings. The police got wind of the meeting only after it was over, and they arrested Shiv Prasad Gupta.

Soon after, the India League sent a delegation to India to enquire into police atrocities and political repression in the country. The Congress Working Committee decided to appoint Jayaprakash as their representative, who would tour the country with the delegation and arrange meetings with the Congress leaders. This was a safeguard against a "conducted tour" being arranged by the British Government, whereby all the trouble spots would be avoided so as not to give the delegation the "wrong" impression.

The Government, however, had other plans for J.P. They issued a warrant for his arrest, and he was picked up in Madras. Rajagopalachari tried to move the High Court with a writ of *habeas corpus*, but J.P. was quickly whisked away to Nasik Jail in the Bombay Province. The Free Press Journal of Bombay ran banner headlines : 'Congress Brain Arrested.'

The *satyagraha* campaign of 1930 had been a spectacular success. The *satyagraha* of 1932, however, was in danger of ending in failure. What had happened ? The Gandhi-Irwin Pact of 1930 had inspired some confidence that Indian nationalist organisations would be allowed to function in full legality. The Congress dropped its defences. But the next Viceroy, Willingdon, took full advantage of this, and a vicious campaign to stamp out the Congress was unleashed. While the *satyagraha* was on, the Government announced special electoral representation for the untouchables. Gandhi responded with a fast unto death unless the award was rescinded. He was released from jail, but the 'untouchable issue' was propelled into national prominence, and public attention shifted from the *satyagraha*.

And so, the *satyagraha* failed. A large number of *satyagrahis* became embroiled in the untouchable issue. Soon after, however, the Congress leaders raised a new slogan—demanding representation in the provincial assemblies and councils. In effect, the policy of Non-cooperation was given up in favour of contesting assembly seats. It was to be a show of strength.

Inside the British Indian jails, however, this new policy caused a lot of concern and some heart-searching. Whole cadres of nationalist youth were still behind bars. They posed some hard questions: after Non-cooperation in 1920-21, and the Civil Disobedience movement in 1930 and 1932, had things come to this pass ? Was the national movement going to compromise its methods ? Wherever they were, in jails in Patna, Lucknow, Lahore or Nasik, these young politicians came to a single conclusion: Gandhi had played his cards and lost and that he had taken them as far as he was capable of doing—but from now on, they had to go it alone. With this attitude, they formulated a critique of Gandhi's methods, and they concluded that a purely political movement had to be buttressed by an economic programme. As a promise, political independence was not enough—for whom would there be an independent India and who would benefit from Independence, this had to be defined. As long as the commercial and industrial classes led the national movement, there would be compromises, hesitancy, and the fateful attraction of the ballot-box, so the young politicians argued. It was a Marxist programme —'let us appeal to those who have nothing to lose but their chains.'

In every (political) jail in the country, this new radicalism was fomenting. But most importantly, in Nasik Jail. A select band of young men prepared the ground—Minoo Masani, Achyut Patwardhan, Asoka Mehta, N.G. Gore, S.M. Joshi,

Professor M.L. Dantwala, and Jayaprakash Narayan.

The guiding spirits in other jails were Acharya Narendra Dev, Dr. Ram Monohar Lohia, Dr. Sampurnanand, Meherally, Purushottam Vikramdas, Nanasahib Gore, Ganga Sharan Singh, Nabhakrishna Chaudhuri, Faridual Haq Ansari, Damodar Swarup Seth, Kamladevi Chattopadhyay, K.K. Menon, Surendranath Dwivedi, Munshi Ahmed Deen, Shivnath Bannerjee and many others.

Their new political programme attracted supporters outside jail. Discussions were held; heart-searching was begun. A new middle class revolutionary consciousness was born. And within the Congress, a more radical solution to Civil Disobedience found adherents.

The peasants and industrial workers had to be drawn into the movement, *kisan sabhas* formed, *mazdoor sanghs* organised. The Congress had to woo them, coax them, show them what they had to gain from independence. And once this was accomplished, no force, not even British imperialism, would be capable of resisting. And then ? A Peasants and Workers' State !

J.P. played a very important role in the formulation of this new programme, primarily because he alone had been schooled in orthodox Marxism. Masani was a 'bourgeois democrat.' Acharya Narendra Dev was looking for a compromise between Marx and the Buddha. And these two were regarded as the 'intellectuals.' Dr. Lohia was exploring another route, a synthesis of Gandhi and Marx. Achyut Patwardhan had walked into the movement with a spiritual cast of mind, and Kamladevi was almost abusive about Lenin. Asoka Mehta was the youngest of them all—he admired Stalin, but was somehow also an existentialist. Sampurnanand was a Hindu before he was anything else, self-styled inheritor of Tilak's mantle, and believed in astrology and brute force. (Later, in 1937, he left the party and joined the Government).

And so, the cry went up—Socialists Awake ! From the dark cells to elegant drawing-rooms and coffee cups. It was indeed a strange kind of socialism, for amid the militant rhetoric there was talk of the Vedas and Upanishads, of Rama and the Buddha. And a motley crowd of men too; all of

them were Congressmen. They were anti-Stalin, with garland-
ed pictures of Lenin on their walls . . . . Socialism ? Inside the
Congress ? To understand this, we have to go back a little.

In America, Jayaprakash had familiarised himself with a
large body of Marxist and socialist writing—the classical
texts, as well as those numerous works that followed in the hot
flush of the revolution in Russia. Marx and Engels, as well as
Lenin. After the October Revolution, a Workers' and Peasants' State became a reality. But 'internationalism,' that other
postulate of Marxism, was still a concept, a goal, and towards that end, the Third International (or Comintern) was
formed in Soviet Russia. An isolated communist State clearly
would not do—there had to be a league of such States for
communism to survive in a hostile world.

In 1921, during the Non-cooperation movement, a number
of young Indian agitators went to Russia. Prominent among
them were M.N. Roy, Shivnath Bannerjee and Shaukat
Usmani. At the sessions of the Comintern, these young men
had an opportunity to witness the cut and thrust of current
internationalist thinking, and the brilliant polemics of the
leaders of the Revolution. When they returned to India, they
immediately got busy organising discussion groups to spread
the socialist gospel among workers and intellectuals. The
Meerut Conspiracy Case of 1927 was an inevitable corollary
to their activities—many of them were arrested or expelled
from the country.

In Russia, the Comintern split down the middle, with Stalin
and Trotsky leading rival factions contending for power after
Lenin's death. Towards the end of Lenin's life, Trotsky had
been his right-hand man and a trusted lieutenant. None of
the Russian leaders had inherited Lenin's mantle but Trotsky
came closest to sharing his views. Trotsky was the man who
saw that internationalism could only become a reality through
the individual national revolutions which would create a
community of socialist States. The Comintern, he argued,
either had to support national revolutions or else cease to play
any useful function. Stalin's ascendancy, however, reversed
this policy. Under him, the Comintern became merely a tail
of the Russian Party bureaucracy, which wagged only when
it suited the foreign policy of the Soviet State. From "inter-

nationalism", the theory and practice of communism shifted towards the thesis of "Socialism in one State". Revolution in other nations would have to wait until the Soviet state dug its heels in.

In the light of its new policy, the Comintern analysed the Indian situation thus : the Congress was a "reactionary" organisation, and Gandhi merely a "bourgeois" leader.

The reaction in India to the lack of sympathy from the Soviets was bitter. In an editorial for his paper, *Janata*, Ramvriksh Benipuri wrote : 'The height of foolishness and treachery was reached when, in 1930 and 1932, Indian nationalism was locked in a life and death struggle with English colonialism, and Stalin's agents—who called themselves communists—incited simple-minded workers, attacked patriots, snatched their *tirangas* (Indian national flag) from their hands and burnt them. The police and the communists attacked nationalists in the same manner and together. In this manner, Indian communism and British imperialism went hand in hand.'

In March 1929, Acharya Narendra Dev penned an article in the *Vidyapeeth Newsletter* entitled 'Soviet Russia's Policy in Asia' wherein he observed that for a Bolshevik, the political principles of Bolshevism were of primary importance—all else irrelevant. Soviet Russia was an opponent of nationalism—if it extended its support to an Independence movement, then it was only for the reason that thereby imperialism would suffer a setback and Bolshevism gain a new field to take root and grow in.

At the time Narendra Dev wrote this, he was probably unaware of the resolutions of the Communist International of November 1928, for he did not mention them at all. But by January, 1930 when Jayaprakash met him for the first time, he had sharpened his attitued towards the hardening policy of 'Socialism In One State'—and had become a bitter critic of Soviet colonial and foreign policy, as also of Stalin's leadership.

Of this first meeting, Jayaprakash wrote : 'Soon after my acquaintance with Acharyaji, I began work in the offices of the All-India Congress Committee. A few months later, the Salt *satyagraha* campaign was launched. Acharyaji and I were involved in different spheres of work for the movement. Later in 1933, while we were interned at Nasik Road Central Jail, a few of us formed the idea of launching the Congress Socialist Party. After our release, I talked to the sympathisers at Kashi, and then, on behalf of the Bihar Socialist Party (which had been formed earlier), we summoned an All-India Conference, and sent invitations at all those Congressmen whom we knew to have socialist leanings. The Conference was to take place at Patna'.

Acharya Narendra Dev was to preside over the Conference.

But we have gone too far ahead . . .

A large number of peasants participated in the Civil Disobedience movenment of 1930. Some of them had gone on to play an influential role in the Youth Congress organisa-tions of the time. By 1931, the Congress had included in its Fundamental Principles, the question of Land Reforms and, in particular, the rationalisation of agricultural rents. Marxism fast gathered a corps of young adherents within the Congress. Soon after the first Civil Disobedience movement, a few *satyagrahis* got together and organised a Socialist Union at Patna. Its leading figures were Ganga Sharan Singh, Ramvriksh Benipuri and Phoolan Prasad Varma.

After 1931, international politics revolved around the divergent pulls of three main political trends : in England, the Conservative Government ; the Nazis and Fascists in Germany and Italy ; and the Bolshevik movement nurtured in Soviet Russia. In a sense, this constellation of forces was mirrored in the Indian political arena too. Gandhi espoused a 'Christian' socialism ; but we also had our Bolsheviks, and in Patel and his followers, a conservative force.

Gandhi's 'socialism' was untried, it had not been put to the test anywhere. But it was a creative political atmosphere, and new political forms were spawned with every twist of the national movement. At the Lahore Congress of 1930, Nehru even outlined a political platform that steered midway bet-ween Gandhi and Marx, and drew its inspiration from both. The attempt was somewhat premature, however—nationhood, independence, was the real issue, and socialism was seen, by many, as an unnecessary diversion.

1931 was a fateful year. It was the year of the Depression, and capitalist civilisation seemed in grave danger of collapse. The newspapers reported Hunger Marches in the streets of London ; the price of gold plummeted, unemployment soared. A nagging doubt arose: Germany, England, America, these were free nations, in full control over their own economies. Why then had this great crisis overtaken them ?

It became clear as dawn that self-government was not the great cure it was made out to be. Gandhi was wrong. *Swaraj* would not be enough.

The entire might of the British Empire was pitted against Bolshevism. But Soviet Russia stood firm. While the capitalist economies crashed, the Soviets girded themselves round with steel mills, iron foundries, heavy industry. The doubt persisted: had India, in its nationalism, and also its traditionalism, neglected to consider the Soviet alternative ?

J.P. was one of those Indian political workers who were assailed by this doubt, and converted it into a new political programme. And he went beyond the moderate Socialist thinkers of his day, and beyond men like Ramsay Mac-Donald, the British Labour leader.

At the session of the Lahore Congress, J.P. developed his ideas and put them before the delegates. He compared that session with the one held at Bombay in 1919. He reminded them of a historic resolution, 'At Bombay, it was said—"We must bring about change. Reform will not do." ' He reiterated the question of economic autonomy first mooted at Karachi. India had been a slave so long that people had forgotten what freedom is, or why it was desired.

In 1931, J.P.'s was a lone voice. But soon after, Jawaharlal Nehru became a comrade-in-arms.

Gandhi's movement flared up. J.P. was in jail until 1933. In jail, he reflected and reconsidered. During those two years, Hitler rose to power in Germany. Nehru cautioned the Congressmen against Hitler's brand of 'socialism'.

After this brooding spell in jail, 1933 was a decisive year. Gandhi's *satyagraha* of that year faltered and was quashed. It did not seem to have achieved any thing at all. In the Congress, the clamour for contesting assembly seats grew louder: the Non-cooperation movement seemed at an end. To top it all, Gandhi dissociated himself from the movement. These events had a decisive influence on J.P. His conversion from a social democrat to a socialist was completed.

The example of Germany was a factor in J.P.'s disillusionment with social democracy. Hitler had risen to power over the dead bodies of the parliamentary parties. Parliament was helpless—it had stood by, and now, had become a mockery of itself. In Germany and in Spain, the socialists were forced to be on the defensive. Thousands perished. J.P. wrote : 'No foreign government can make a 'gift' of parliamentary democracy to a subject nation. Such institutions evolve out of nationalism, and the organised revolutionary struggles of the working-class. Revolutionary workers and peasants and revolutionary nationalists must cooperate towards the overthrow of imperialism. Separately, one without the other, they will achieve nothing.'

J.P. himself was both a nationalist and a socialist—he identified with the working class, and he was a fierce nationalist. But the formulation was not merely apt—it applied to the situation of a country at a critical stage of struggle. It was, moreover, an original contribution to Marxist thought.

A party was formed. They called it the Congress Socialist Party. Its leader was Jayaprakash Narayan. The name of the party represented its twin identity. It was 'Congress' in so far as it shared the militant nationalism of the Congress Party. True, nationalism in a free country could well be a reactionary rallying cry. But in a colony, it always is a revolutionary sentiment, subversive of imperialism. As J.P. said, 'Socialism cannot advance in our country, without allying itself with revolutionary nationalism.'

Clearly, what irked J.P. most was the attitude of the Indian Bolsheviks towards the national movement, and his conception of the Congress Socialist Party was a corrective to their hostile attitude. Not only had the Bolsheviks, in accordance with Comintern directives, stayed aloof from the movement, they had labelled it a 'bourgeois' movement. J.P. felt they were mis-applying Marxist theory to suit the requirements of Soviet foreign policy. Indian Socialism had to go it alone, without the Bolsheviks, without the Comintern.

The need of the hour was for a socialist party that would participate in the wider arena of the nationalist movement; it would work to channelise nationalist energies towards the inevitable conflict with British imperialism; and when the movement flagged, as it did after the *satyagraha* of 1933, it would help to prevent the struggle from disintegration, and arrest the tendency towards Council-participation. In J.P.'s eyes, the move towards contesting seats on the Provincial Assemblies was nothing short of a compromise with the aims of the movement.

At the same time, it was also hoped of the new party, that it would draw workers and peasants into the movement. The question, 'Nationhood for whom ?' was posed. The Congress socialists answered : 'For the peasants and workers of India.'

The response, within the Congress, to the scheme of a new Party, was encouraging. Quite a number of prominent leaders were enthusiastic. Among them were Jawaharlal Nehru, and Acharya Narendra Dev.

Benipuri has described one of the reactions to the new Party : 'The communists sneered at the fusion of nationalism and socialism, and said that whereas the socialists in Bihar merely added the name 'Congress' to their organisation, others within the Congress adopted the word 'socialist' to their names. But Jayaprakash has affirmed that the Party cannot be a Socialist Party alone, but a Congress Socialist Party, whereby we do not lose sight of the historic role of the Congress. The twelve years of its existence has affirmed the importance of this insight. Despite the fact that Stalin's Indian agents poked fun at the name, and drew a parallel with Hitler's 'National Socialists,' many of them later joined the Party, and a great number were expelled for indiscipline.'

J.P. and his associates decided to invite all those with socialist leanings, to help in launching the new Party and forming an All-India Socialist forum. The need to arrest the Congress defeatism, its participation in election, was announced as an objective. The necessity of disbanding all the tiny, rival workers' bodies, and uniting in a single and powerful Trade Union Congress was announced. Similarly, the need for *kisan sabhas* that would represent the entire country and the need to promote a socialist discipline and consciousness among students and the younger generation were also stressed.

A huge conference was summoned. Then suddenly, on the afternoon of the 15th of January, 1934, Bihar was rocked by a devastating earthquake. Monghyr and Muzaffarpur were the worst affected areas. The nation turned its attention towards the calamity.

Help came from abroad too. Money, blankets, clothes were made available. But the biggest need was for a volunteer task force to help in housing the victims of the earthquake, the injured and the homeless. A relief centre was organised at Patna. After his release from jail, J.P. came to Patna, and became an official at the Relief Centre. It was the first time since his return, that he had an opportunity to do any work within Bihar. He had become totally unfamiliar with the trends of political activity among Bihar's youth. But now, working for the Earthquake Relief Centre, he was in a position to meet hundreds of young people, to estimate their potential for political work. He then decided that from that time onwards Bihar would be his field of operations.

To voluntary workers in the programme, the relief work was an eye-opener. The assistance that was given to the poor farmers and farm-labourers was promptly diverted to the landlords' coffers. The *zamindari* system was seen in its most rapacious, unrelenting form when, peasants were forced to pay exorbitant prices even for the thatch and bamboo which they needed to build new huts. The *zamindars* made no concessions, there was no let-up in their inordinate greed.

Jayaprakash joined the Bihar Socialist Party and utilised this entree to persuade his fellow-members to join the All-India Congress Socialist Party Union. Soon after, Bihar was electrified by the news that the All-India Congress Committee was scheduled to be held at Patna. Gandhi was to address the delegates on the subject of withdrawing the *satyagraha*, and the 'Co-operators' within the Congress would put forward the case for returning to the Councils and Assemblies. It was an opportune time for rallying all those who felt that the Congress was losing its bite and succumbing to the lure of office. The Bihar Socialist Party went ahead and invited delegates from all parts of the country for a mammoth Socialist Conference. And out of this Conference was born the

Congress Socialist Pary as a formal body.

The delegates met on the 17th May, 1934, at the Anjuman Islamia Hall in Patna. Acharya Narendra Dev took the chair with about one hundred delegates attending, and the proceedings started. The majority sentiment seemed against any move which might amount to a revival of the Swaraj Party. Not everyone was opposed to Council-entry. The delegates from Bombay thought that the purpose of the meeting was to select socialist-minded candidates to represent the Congress in the Assembly elections ! In fact, the meeting had a less specific, but a more important matter to consider. The All-India Congress Committee was to meet the next day, and the Socialists had to hammer out a policy, and to agree upon an attitude towards the Congress. The aim was to present the Congress with a well-defined programme, backed by a phalanx of left-wing Congressmen and socialists. Two tangible issues were : Council entry and the revival of the Swaraj Party.

Gandhi was known to be warming towards the Swaraj Party. Soon after he had withdrawn the *satyagraha*, he had attended a meeting on the 31st March, 1934 in Delhi, which was ostensibly an attempt to rake the ashes of Swarajist organisation that had died in 1930. A few other prominent leaders who attended were : Bhulabhai Desai, K.M. Munshi, Dr. M.A. Ansari, and Sir P.C. Ray.

Jawaharlal Nehru was interned at the Naini Jail at the time of the meeting in Patna, and therefore, could not attend the session. Jayaprakash and Narendra Dev were the principal figures. At the end of a long round of discussions, summing up the proceedings, Acharya Narendra Deva (as Chairman) said : 'For a subject, colonial State, political independence is the first step on the road to socialism. In a middle-class revolutionary movement, for socialism to stay away from the nationalist movement would be fatal. It is also essential, for the success of the national movement, to base itself upon the support of the people together with the middle-class. The economic well-being of the common people must, however, find a central place in the programme of the movement. The Congress Socialist Party must not divorce the National Movement from the revolutionary aspirations of workers, peasants and the middle-class.'

The exchange of views during the discussion also established what conditions the delegates considered to be 'ripe' for socialism. Basing their views on the Russian example, they felt that an economically depressed nation, indusrially underdeveloped, but capable of generating a revolutionary mass movement, was most likely to undergo a socialist transformation.

The Conference also turned its attention to the international situation, in particular, to the storm-clouds of Fascism looming on the horizon. The possibility of an imminent European war was discussed, and the Conference agreed that in such an event, the British Empire should not be supported by the nationalists. Soviet Russia was discussed—and also the progress of Socialist Reconstruction in that country. The delegates also expressed their concern about constitutionalism in the Congress, and agreed that the only way to win freedom was on the barricades. A significant consensus had been achieved.

Finally, the Conference decided to regularise their meetings by calling an All-India Socialist Party into being. Narendra Dev was appointed to head a committe to draft a constitution and programme for the Party. Jayaprakash was appointed to head the organisational wing of the new Party. And immediately, the Congress was presented with a list of demands, which were the affirmation of the following objectives and principles: the establishment of a working-class state; planned economic development; the nationalisation of major industries and productive enterprises; state control of foreign trade; the abolition of the status and privileges of princes and zamindars; re-distribution of land; encouragement of state and collective farming; a moratorium on peasant indebtedness; and a firm commitment to democratic principles.

In his capacity as general secretary, Jayaprakash toured the country, and set up branches of the Party in all the major Provinces. The first regular meeting of the new Party was held in Bombay in 1934. Sampurnanand presided. The second meeting took place at Meerut, in 1936, this time with Kamladevi Chattopadhyay as President; the third in

December 1937 at Faizpur, Jayaprakash presiding; the fourth
at Lahore in December 1938, with Minoo Masani presiding.
During all these years, however, it was Jayaprakash who
relentlessly campaigned and shouldered the onus of the organisational work. In more ways than one, it was Jayaprakash
more than any other leader, who left his stamp on the
character of the Party.

What, indeed, was the 'character' of the Party ? The thesis,
propounded at the Meerut session provides a clear elucidation.
It said :

The Congress Socialist Party grew out of the experience
of the last two national struggles. When the last *satyagraha*
came to an end, some Congressmen felt that the national
movement be given a new direction and purpose. Its aims
and objectives needed to be formulated afresh, and new
tactics devised. The lead was given by those people who
understood the theory and correctly assessed the nature and
place of the working classes in the current political situation.
It was thus natural that the new Party would be Socialist.
The word 'Congress', that was part of the title, attested to
the Party's affiliation to the nationalist struggle . . . .

Jayaprakash Narayan has written :

The objects of the Congress Socialist Party, laid down
in its Constitution, are 'the achievement of complete
independence, in the sense of separation from the British
Empire, and the establishment of a socialist society.'

This is direct and simple enough. The Party has two
objects : the first is the same as that of the Indian National
Congress, except that the Party wishes to make it clear that
the complete independence of India must include separation
from the British Empire.

The second object of the Party means that Independent
India must recognise its economic life on a socialist basis.
Why?

The question at bottom is one of values and ultimate
objectives, which once determined, the rest becomes a
matter of logical sequence.

If the ultimate objective is to make the masses politically
and economically free, to make them prosperous and happy,

to free them from all manner of exploitation, to give them
unfettered opportunity for development, then, socialism
becomes a goal to which one must irresistibly be drawn. If
again, the objective is to take hold of the chaotic and coflic-
ting forces of society and to fashion the latter according to
the ideal of utmost social good and to harness of all conscious directives of human intelligence in the service of the
commonwealth, then, again, socialism becomes an inescap-
able destination.

If, then, these be our objectives, it should take little
argument, to show that socialism is as definitely 'indicated'
in India as elsewhere. In India too there is poverty, nay,
starvation, on the one hand and wealth and luxury on the
other : in India too there is exploitation; the means of
production here also are in private hands. That is, the root
evil of modern society, namely, economic and social inequa-
lity exists in India too as does its cause—the exploitation of
the great many by the very few.

And this is not the result of British rule. It is independent of it and will continue even after it. The ending of the
foreign domination would not automatically solve India's
problem of poverty, would not put a stop to the exploitation of the vast many, would not in fact, mean the accomp-
lishment of any of the objectives which we have started
with. Economic freedom is also indispensable.

By the end of the Meerut Conference, J.P. had formulated his criticism of the Congress :

The present programme of the Congress falls far short
of these ideals. It might ameliorate the conditions of the
masses to a certain extent, but it will neither rid them of
exploitation nor put them in power. Far from effecting
revolutionary changes in it, it leaves the economic structure
of society intact. It leaves capitalists, landlords and princes
on one side and workers, tenants and subjects on the other.
It leaves the means of production in the hands of private
individuals, except in the sphere of key industries. The
entire economic organisation, based as it is on the exploitation of the poor and middle classes, is preserved. This is
not economic freedom. The preamble and substance of the

Karachi Resolution are at wide variance with each other. What we endeavour to do is to remove this variance and bring them close together. When the Congress professes the economic freedom of the masses, let it distinctly state what that freedom means.

The Congress may be unprepared for the acceptance of such a minimum programme as we advocate. But it is one thing to say that we are not ready for any further definition of our goal—which of course may be disputed—and quite another, as latterly repeated *ad nauseam* that socialism is moonshine; that it is unsuited to the Indian climate; that Indian socialists are merely adventuring in the realm of theory; that they are only quoting a rusty old German Jew who called himself Karl Heinrich Marx; and the rest of the drivel.

The Socialists did not insist that the Congress accept their programme wholesale. But what was crucial to their endeavour was to try and influence the Congress to accept a minimum economic programme which would release millions of people from economic bondage when Independence came.

The full statement of the aims of the C.S.P., as written into their constitution, read as follows:

1) Transfer of all power to the producing masses;
2) Development of the economic life of the country to be planned and controlled by the State;
3) Socialisation of key and principal industries (e.g., Steel, Cotton, Jute, Railways), Shipping, Plantations, Mines, Banks, Insurance and Public Utilities, with a view to the progressive socialisation of all the instruments of production, distribution and exchange;
4) State monopoly of foreign trade;
5) Organisation of co-operatives for production, distribution and credit in the unsocialised sector of economic life;
6) Elimination of princes and landlords and all other classes of exploiters without compensation;
7) Redistribution of land to peasants;
8) Encouragement and promotion of co-operative and collective farming by the State;

9) Liquidation of debts owed by peasants and workers;
10) Recognition of the right to work or maintenance by the State;
11) "To every one according to his needs and from every one according to his capacity" to be the basis ultimately of distribution and production of economic goods;
12) Adult franchise on a functional basis;
13) No support to or discrimination between religions by the State and no recognition of any distinction based on caste or community;
14) No discrimination between the sexes by the State;
15) Repudiation of the so-called Public Debt of India.

These were the fifteen planks in the Congress Socialist Party's platform. At first glance, the demands are very high-sounding and pompous, the phrases seem articulated with a foreign accent. In fact, however, the programme is quite simple—all the objectives are quite attainable, given the will to realise them. As for the foreign-sounding phrases, are not the mills and factories, the railways that span the entire country, the constituent assemblies and legislative councils, are not they all importations from a foreign political-industrial culture ?

J.P. wrote : '(This programme is) intended to establish the rather simple principle . . . . of abolition of private ownership, of functional property, which, as we saw, was the real villain of the piece—the source of all our evils, or most of them. This is further intended to establish the most eminently reasonable of principles of social life—social planning.'

The central offices of the Party were set up at Kashi (Benares). As "Prime Minister" of the Party, J.P., together with Acharya Narendra Dev, undertook the management of the Party activities.

J.P. has given us a succint account of how the socialists, while remaining within the Congress, intended to function:

Our work within the Congress is governed by the policy of developing it into a true anti-imperialist body. It is not our purpose, as sometimes it has been misunderstood to be, to convert the whole Congress into a full-fledged socialist party. All we seek to do is to change the content and policy of that organisation that it comes truly to represent the masses, having the object of emancipating them both from the foreign power and the native system of exploitation.

There are some who ridicule this whole idea. Their view is that the Congress is a bourgeois body with absolutely no chance of being influenced in the direction I have indicated. We do not subscribe to this view. The Congress at present is dominated by upper class interests and its leaders are uncompromisingly opposed to admitting into its objectives any programme aimed at the economic emancipation of the masses. Yet, within the Congress there is a very large body of opinion which would welcome such a programme. Only, this body which had worked under the old leadership has to be convinced that the programme we advocated will not weaken the national struggle by dividing, as they have learnt to think, the nationalist forces. If we seek to influence them—and without influencing them no group of pure and brilliant theorists can develop an anti-imperialist movement in this country—it is not sufficient to abuse the leadership or to produce learned theses. What is need is a demonstration in actual practice that our programme is more dynamic and effective.

The whole story of the Congress Socialist participation in the Congress would take up an entire book on its own. Here, we can only briefly describe the twelve years of the C.S.P.'s existence.

Within the Congress, the Party's work could be divided under four heads :

1) The campaign against participation in the Council of the British Raj;

2) Drawing the attention of the Congress towards the economic plight of the people;

3) The attempt to resolve some of the organisational deficiencies in the Congress Party; and

4) Keeping the Congress in militant opposition to the Raj.

The years 1933 to 1936 were an important time in J.P.'s life—the years when his youthful exuberance blossomed into full-blown manhood. In this period he wrote a book called

Why Socialism, which was published by the All-India Congress Socialist Party, Benares. In this work, he developed four important theses :
1) The foundations of socialism.
2) What the Congress Socialist stands for.
3) Alternatives.
4) Methods and techniques.

At the age of thirty-two, he attained nation-wide stature through this revolutionary document. He demonstrated in this book that parting company with the Comintern and the Indian Bolshevik line in no way entailed a disenchantment with Marxism. On the contrary, he argued that only the Congress Socialist Party and its supporters were successfully paving the way for Marxism in the Indian situation. 'Socialism', he said, 'has a single form, and a single principle, and that is Marxism.' It was true, he said, that separate socialist parties disagreed about methods and tactics—so far, only the Bolsheviks in Russia had successfully staged a revolution, thereby commanding great respect for their tactical line. Their success was proof that their methods had been correct for Russia—but not necessarily for the whole world. Socialism, he said, is a method of building a new society. If a group of idealists without authority or power wanted to wish socialism into existence, they would not be able to do so. 'No party can build up socialism unless it has the machinery of the State in its hands; whether it has come to acquire it through the will of the electorate or by a *coup d'etat* is irrelevant . . . . The coercive powers of a socialist State, if they exist at all, are bound to be derived from popular support.'

Why Socialism also dealt with the reasons for the uneven distribution of wealth, which, he said, stemmed from the fact that a few people established a monopoly over the natural resources and the means of production. Hence, if a government wanted to put an end to shortages and disparities, the answer was to put an end to private ownership of the means of production and allow society to collectively enjoy the fruits of production.

J.P. dealt extensively with the *raison d'etre* of the Congress Socialist Party, what it was and why it was formed. First, he

refuted the contention that it was impossible to bring socialism to India because her cultural traditions differed from
Europe, and because industrially India was an infant.
'It is often said that India's conditions are peculiar . . . . If
by this it is meant that the basic principles of socialism have
no validity in India, it would be difficult to imagine a greater
fallacy. The laws by which wealth accumulates hold as true
in India as elsewhere and the manner in which this accumula-
tion can be stopped is the same here as elsewhere.'

J.P. described the fifteen planks in the C.S.P.'s platform as
essential steps towards a socialist society, culled and derived
from a Marxist blueprint. But there were also glimpses of
J.P.'s personal contribution to the programme, adaptions
where European Marxism would not apply to the Indian conditions, changes where the Russian example had indicated
errors of judgment, such as the question of State and collective farming. Here J.P. envisaged the basic unit of production
as the single village, instead of groups of villages as had been
tried in Soviet Russia. The result would be like the village
communes of ancient India, with the difference that, instead of
being an isolated, separate entity, the socialist village would
be an essential part of the wider economic, co-operative
system. In addition, in India, the transition to State and
collective farming would be gradual and orderly, in contrast
to the Soviet example. Again, unlike the Soviets, force as a
means of establishing this type of farming would be eschewed.
Because of her huge population and the shortage of culti-
vable land, India would not need labour-saving agricultural
implements urgently. Cities would be planned—socialist cities.
Industry would be divided up so as to prevent centralisation,
and unbalanced concentration in one place. And in this
manner J.P. based his vision of the socialist future on a
conception of the agro-industrial village.

Inevitably, as the socialist blue-print took shape, and the
tactical line was formulated, the concern with the most
immediate objective—Independence—was sharpened. Although
J.P. had played a crucial role in laying the foundations of
the C.S.P. in the conviction that the Indian Bolsheviks were
wrong in their non-involvement with the nationalist movement, nevertheless he nurtured a dream that socialists and

Bolsheviks would one day bury their differences and unite in pursuance of their common objective of establishing a socialist society. In 1936, there seemed a real possibility that this dream would become a reality, when the Comintern adopted a new attitude towards the Indian situation. Despite this re-assessment, however, the coalition of the two parties did not take place.

Jawaharlal Nehru too was a socialist and friendly towards the socialists within the Congress. He was also, of course, J.P.'s *bhai* (brother and comrade). In 1934, when the C.S.P. was beginning to harden into an organisation, Nehru was in the jail and played no part in the launching of the party. When he was released, he did not seek to be formally associated with the C.S.P., thereby disappointing a great many of his admirers, but not J.P. Nehru remained in sympathy with the rationale of the party's foundation, which was to push the Congress towards socialism. Nevertheless, he felt that the C.S.P. was being too derivative in its Western rhetoric and that it could be too difficult for the common people to under-stand its programme. Further, he did not like the idea of a clique. Its membership did not encompass anyone who was not a member of the Congress. But perhaps Nehru's biggest reason for not joining the C.S.P. was that in a way he was a politician par excellence. Acutely aware of the levers of power, he knew that by retaining the image of a leader of national stature, he stood a better chance of making socia-lism respectable, and smuggling it into the Congress.

Nehru also knew that by joining the C.S.P., he would lose Gandhi's support, and thereby would jeopardise his political future.

In 1936, Jawaharlal was the President of the Congress session held at Lucknow. The strange fact is that despite his lukewarm attitude towards the C.S.P., he co-opted three socialists into the Congress Working Committee—Acharya Narendra Dev, Jayaprakash Narayan and Achyut Patwardhan. The front page of the *Bombay Chroncile*, 17th April 1936, announced, 'Socialists in the Congress Working Committee'. The Committee was composed thus :

President : Jawaharlal Nehru
Treasurer : Seth Jamnalal Bajaj

General Secretary : Acharya J.B. Kripalani

Members : Maulana Azad, Rajendra Prasad, Acharya Narendra Dev, Jayaprakash Narayan, Achyut Patwardhan, Patel, Khan Abdul Ghafoor Khan, Rajagopalachari, Subhas Chandra Bose, Jayramdas Daulatram, Shankar Rao Dev, and Bhulabhai Desai.

Only two members of the Working Committee were not members of the A.I.C.C.—Jayaprakash and Rajaji. According to the rules of the Congress Constitution, only members of the latter body were eligible for membership of the Working Committee. For this reason, Nehru had the rule amended at the Lucknow Congress. The new Working Committee met at Wardha on the 27th April that year at three o'clock in the afternoon. J.P.'s place as the General Secretary of the C.S.P. was taken by Masani.

From the Lucknow Congress and the Wardha session, and through the next four or five months, J.P. and Jawaharlal were very close to each other. J.P. assured him that great changes in the Congress were expected, and that the hope of a number of people were pinned on Jawaharlal. The older and more conservative leaders in the Congress were not at all pleased at the place of honour which the socialists had carved out for themselves. There were frequent clashes. Nehru was utterly dismayed, and even went so far as to consider resigning from the Congress. In these times of personal travail, J.P. moved even closer to Jawaharlal Nehru.

Eventually, matters came to the boil in June 1936, at the end of which seven members of the Working Committee sent in their resignation. Rajendra Prasad, Sardar Patel and Rajaji were among these seven. J.P. and Gandhi got to work soothing ruffled feelings, and the resignation letters were rescinded or withdrawn.

At the root of all these conflicts were the three socialists, chiefly Jayaprakash, whose *raison d'etre* was to give the Congress a leftward direction.

But because J.P. valued the continued existence of the Congress as an essential nationalist organisation, he decided to put an end to the clashes by resigning from the Working Committee, six months after he had joined it. Those six months had been a painful eye-opener for him. For the

Congress, he said, socialism was merely an article of faith;
for the C.S.P., however, it was a creed—and hence the
differences. Unfortunately, not Nehru but the Old Guard, led
by Patel, controlled the Working Committee, and these men
were neither socialists nor full-fledged secularists.

The resignation letter had first to go to Nehru. At the end
of July that year, J.P. wrote him a personal letter. Nehru
replied on the 7th of August, 1936 :

My dear Jayaprakash,

*Your letter reached me towards the end of July. It was
not possible for me to reply to it except by telegram. I
did not know what to say in a telegram. Just then my mind
was in a kind of daze owing to the continuous touring and
engagements. I was unable to think clearly and so I refrained from sending you a telegram. I am yet unable to give
you an opinion because I have not the data with me. On the
facts as I know them I should have liked you to continue but
it's so extraordinarily difficult to advise in such matters where
personal considerations crop up. However it seems that you
have already taken that step (resignation from the Working
Committee) and we must face it. It adds to the complexity
of the situation and I do not quite know what will happen. . . .
I should like to meet you before I go to Bombay.*

Yours affectionately,
Jawaharlal

At the time, J.P. would receive his mail through the
offices of the *Searchlight*. Nehru sent his letter at this address.
J.P. was touring the country, recruiting members for his
Party, establishing chapter and branch organisations in fresh
towns. These were long and tiring journeys, meeting thousands of people, speechifying, arguing, explaining to large
audiences. There was no respite during the tours; in between
the hectic programmes, J.P. was also busy with his writing,
organising socialist book clubs, collecting funds for the
Party, planning out study camps, bringing out leaflets and
newsletters, formulating resolutions for the Party's considera-
tion. He also had to keep up a steady stream of correspond-

ence to ensure that the Congress workers, particularly Jawaharlal Nehru, were not weaned away from their leftward inclinations.

J.P.'s travels took him to all parts of the country. Generally he travelled third class. If he was going a long distance, he went by what was then known as railway 'inter class.' Most of his travelling was by rail, or else by car, Sometimes, he travelled by bullock-cart and even riding an elephant. Often where there were no roads, he had to go on foot through kutcha tracks in mud and slush.

Against his own inclinations, and bending to the will of the Congress Working Committee and Gandhi, Nehru agreed to explore the possibility of working the Constitution of 1935, and to fight the elections. Under the provisions of the 1935 Act, most of the British Indian provinces were to have a bicameral legislative of directly elected representatives of the people. Elections to the assemblies were scheduled for February 1937. The C.S.P. put up candidates to publicise the Party's programme, and gave its support to the Congress. The Congress won a thumping victory, and suddenly, within its ranks, a conclave in favour of forming a Ministry stood forth. To this step, the C.S.P was bitterly opposed. The denouement came when, at the Delhi session of the A.I.C.C., there was a clear majority in favour of taking office.

The Ministries were formed: but political prisoners, offenders against the Raj, continued to languish in jails. Here was a great opportunity to point out the anomaly of accepting responsibility without effective power. J.P. raised a powerful slogan : 'Release (the prisoners) or Resign', which forced the Ministries in the then United Provinces and Bihar to resign. The British authorities took fright, and released the prisoners, to save the remaining Ministries from this test.

From this point on, the Congress and its Socialist embryo began to drift apart. The C.S.P. had always been aware of weaknesses in the oraganisation and character of its parent body. In 1935, J.P. had expressed this trend of dissatisfaction in a pamphlet published from Benares :

There is another direction in which we must develop the Congress. This concerns its internal organisation and constitution. The basis of individual membership on which the Congress is at present organised is very unsatisfactory. It becomes an artificial body, representative not of the masses, but of a handful of members. We must endeavour to change this constitution in such a manner as to make the Congress a direct representative of the people. In my view this can best be done by developing a system of group representation. Members who constitute a primary committee of the Congress should be representatives of class and group organisations. They should represent tenants, farmers, labourers, merchants, the professions and so on. The actual details of this plan may be difficult to draw up, but the principle is simple enough, and, to my mind, most just and proper.

One very big reason why the Congress was so successful in the elections of 1937 was the presence of the C.S.P. leftist lobby in its midst, which had caught the imagination of the working class and peasantry throughout the country. Well before the election campaign, J.P. had announced, from the C.S.P. and the Congress platforms, their resolution in favour of land reform. The poorer sections of the peasantry were promised reductions in the rent exacted by landlords. They would be given more time to repay loans, discounts in the rates of repayment, and facilities for fresh loans at low interest rates.

In the hot flush of their victory, the Congress took it into its head to disregard all the other political perties in the field. Nehru went so far as to say : 'The real contest is between two forces—the Congress as representing the road to freedom of the nation, and the British Government of India, and its supporters who oppose and try to suppress this urge....For the Government, there is only one principal opponent—the Congress.' Jinnah had expostulated : 'No, there is a third Party in the conflict—the Muslims.'

But the Congress did not stop at this taunt of Jinnah. During the elections, it tried to negotiate a secret pact with the Muslim League in U.P., whereby a coalition Ministry would be formed if they won. After the results were declared, however, the Congress found it did not need the support of the League. The pact was abrogated, and Jinnah, shocked and disillusioned, raised the cry: 'Islam is in danger'.

It is from this point onwards that the disenchantment of
the Muslim masses with the Congress and the socialist party
led them into the arms of the Muslim League en masse. For
J.P., this was a painful expose of the devious ways in which the
Congress could function. Throughout the years 1937 and
1938, J.P. was busy touring the country, desperately trying to
dispel the air of a political situation that had become suffo-
cating. In June 1938, Nehru visited Europe on the plea that
he needed a 'change of air'. As soon as he returned, in
November of the same year, J.P. sent him a long letter dated
the 23rd November, 1938 from Calicut, which sounded as
though he had been waiting to unburden himself for a long
time :

Dear Bhai,

    *I hasten to add my welcome to that of the nation to you
on your homecoming. I wish it were possible for me to rush
up to Allahabad to meet you and talk to you about the tragic
events that you have witnessed in Europe and about things that
have happened here since you left. I may be able to fulfil
this desire in a couple of weeks if you are not immediately
caught up in a whirlwind programme. I have been vegetating
here in Malabar, undergoing a special Ayurvedic treatment
for my sciatica. I feel better though not cured. Prabhavati is
with me. It gave us great pleasure to read in the papers that
you are much improved in health as a result of your European
tour.*

    *I hope that having been in the midst of tremendous happen-
ings you have not forgotten the small affair of the Socialist
Book Club of which I wrote to you. We have been able to
make some progress with our scheme, and with the help of
Subhas Babu we were able to raise about Rs. 3,000 for it
at Calcutta. The office of the Club is at Allahabad and
Ahmed is in charge as Managing Director.*

    *The Club is a non-party affair. In the letter you wrote
from Europe you expressed your inability to join the Club as
a foundation member till you had occasion to know more
about it. You had also expressed your reluctance to identify
yourself with any group. As I have said the Club is not a
group affair and has no allegiance to anything except to*

socialist literature . . . . Subhas Babu is already a foundation member of the Club. Your refusal to join it would be a great blow to us. I admit that the Club would work on a small scale, but I think it would be unreasonable to expect from the socialist movement in India results that are beyond its resources. And, if you will excuse me for saying so, it would be unfair of you, who are naturally used to doing things on a grand scale, to non-cooperate with the efforts of socialists in India just because they are puny compared with those of older and wider organisations. We are, I think, not unjustified in expecting that if you will not fully identify with us, you will, as a socialist, at least help us in doing well the little we may undertake to do.

In your letter you had said that politics in India had fallen into a rut. In your absence they have only gone deeper into it. I feel that . . . things are slowly happening which are converting the Congress from a democratic organisation of millions of down-trodden people into a handmaid of vested interests. A vulgarisation of Gandhism makes this transition easy and gives this new Congress the requisite demogogic armour. It seems to me that the need has arisen of examining closely the trend of the Congress policy, particularly in the Congress provinces, and of redefining the socio-economic goals of the Congress. The attitude of the Congress governments towards the Labour movement as represented by the Trade Union Congress should be an eye-opener to those who do not wish that the Ministries should be utilised to bind the workers' organisations hand and foot and deliver them to the employers. We are faced today with the real danger of Indian industry being made a synonym for Indian nationalism.

In the same letter J.P. said that the socialists considered the *kisan sabhas*, the workers' union and youth cadres, all as integral parts of the Congress:

It remains for you to consider what must be done to give shape and firmness to that undoubted urge towards social freedom that exists among the overwhelming majority of the people of this country and also, I believe, of the Congress members. This urge has not found any wider expression yet than that represented by the incipient socialist movement in

*the country. I believe that basic work has to be done for
this purpose and that you alone can do it if you only spared
a little time and thought for it.*

*. . . There remains the immediately more important question
of the next offensive (will it be the last ?) against the enemy.
Have we any clear conception of what we are doing to prepare ourselves for it ? When shall we launch it ? Are we to
wait until the British choose a time for us which will
naturally be more favourable to them. I suppose the technique of* satyagraha *does not permit one to prepare plans of
offensive in advance. The only plan we may conceive of is
that we must spin more and do other soul-stirring things like
that. But will you be satisfied with it ? Practically all that you
added to the Congress programme after such strenuous fights
in the Working Committee have been shelved—the democrati-
sation of the Congress Committees, mass contacts, Muslim
contacts, combating the slave constitution. Of course, there is
a silver lining too—the awakening of the States and it is
heartening that you intend devoting some attention to it. But
the other things need your attention much more . . . .*

With regards,

Yours affectionately,

Jayaprakash

For this period, Prabhavati's diary provides us with a useful
insight into J.P.'s state of mind :

26-8-1934 : Wardha

Today I received a telegram from Jayaprakashji. He has
called me to Patna immediately. Talked to Bapu about
going.

29-8-1934 : Wardha

Bapu explained a lot of things about Jayaprakashji to me,
that I liked very much.

14-9-1934 : Wardha

Talked to Bapu for a long time. He helped me to understand very nicely. Gave me a beautiful lecture. Told me
about himself too. God help me. I feel very restless. I put
my trust in God.

8-10-1934 : Wardha

Jayaprakashji arrived. Today I feel very sad and worried,

and for this reason do not write much. I do not understand what is happening. I meditate on God. Give me peace. During the massage, talked to Bapu a little.

9-10-1934 : *Wardha*

Talked to Bapu. He explained to me very clearly my duty. After that, I listened to Bapu and Jayaprakashji talking.

14-10-1934 : *Wardha*

It was decided that I will stay at the *ashram* for a year under Kakaji's charge. He (J.P.) will give me twenty-five rupees. The *ashram* will supply me food and water. In this way, I will learn to be able to stand on my own feet. After a year, I will go and live with Jayaprakashji.

14-11-1934 : *Wardha*

Received a letter from Jayaprakashji. In the evening, while we were strolling, talked to Bapu. What is my duty with regard to going to Bombay ? Bapu explained.

A further insight into J.P.'s conjugal life is furnished by a few letters from Gandhi to Prabhavati :

Delhi
18.12.1933

Dear Prabha,

I got your letter. Also Jayaprakash's. If both of you have decided that you want to dedicate your lives to seva, *then I have nothing to say. I have explained to both of you that there is no sin in adopting the life of private householders, but if you want to adopt* seva dharma, *then you have to give up your personal* dharma. *If you try to follow both at the same time, there is a danger that you will achieve neither. There will be no difficulty in finding Rs. 50 for Rajeshwar every month. But I am not satisfied with this. What arrangements have you made for your expenses ? What have you done about a loan ? Whatever the conditions are, it will not be said that the real issues are solved. But do not pursue the matter. I do not want to break Jayaprakash's enthusiasm. His intentions are pure. Let us believe that everything will be alright.*

Bapu's blessings

Nandi Hill
19.5.1936

Dear Prabha,

After a long time I received a letter from you today. I have written three letters to you. On the 1st, 12th and 18th. These are quite apart from those I wrote in April. If you have not received any of them, whose fault is it ? But you must admit that I answer every letter you write.

Yes, I met Jayaprakash. We talked. Patwardhan was with us. He did not reply to the letter I wrote him. I thought that he does not want to reply. We talked about your future. He wants you to learn the Montessori method at Kashi for three months, and after that, he would like you to go with him to Patna. He asked for my assent, which I promptly gave him. There is no harm in your learning about Montessori. I am not enamoured of it, but if it is his wish, then you should fulfil it. After that you will stay in Patna or some such place, won't you ? You can discuss this matter with him at length. This is, in essence, what we talked about.

How foolish you are ! You have been unwell, and have not told me about it. Do you still get fits ? What have you done about procuring enough milk for yourself ?

Bapu's blessings

Wardha
30.6.1936

Dear Prabha,

I am tearing up you letter. Why do I want to tear it up ? You seem not to be getting enough sleep, the way your activities are planned. Why can't you sleep easily at night ? What are you worried about ? Go to sleep saying 'Ram, Ram'. It does not seem that you get any sleep during the day either. I got all the news about Patna. It seems you are not fated to be with Jayaprakash and to look after him.

Bapu's blessings

Chapter Four

IN 1936, the symptoms of the coming Second World War were already evident. Different sections of the Indian nationalists were divided in their approach. One point of view was that all advantage should be taken of any difficult situation the British might find themselves in. J.P. disagreed—he did not see why the war was necessary. He called it an imperialist war. But his biggest concern was with the war of Independence.

It was at such time that J.P. dreamt about the union of the Socialist and Bolshevik parties in India. Except Acharya Narendra Dev, none of the other leaders—Dr. Ram Manohar Lohia, Achyut Patwardhan, Asoka Mehta, Minoo Masani—shared J.P.'s enthusiasm about this union. J.P. negotiated a settlement with the Bolsheviks, and they were allowed to join the Congress Socialist Party. But soon after, matters came to a head. In the branches of the C.S.P. in South India, the Bolsheviks soon mustered a majority and Socialists' control over these councils relaxed. It soon became apparent that the Bolsheviks were not really interested in participating in the national movement, but in demonstrating their own power.

As the dark clouds of world war massed on the horizon, J.P. set about strengthening the workers' and peasants' organisations affiliated to his party. At a Party Conference in Bengal, he addressed the meeting with these words :

This process of development of the anti-imperialist forces that I have mentioned just now, cannot be brought about, as I have already said, by mere ideological propa-

ganda. We must at the same time work among the masses.
After all, the anti-imperialist movement will consist not only
of ideologues, but of workers, peasants, the impoverished
middle classes. To work among these classes, to develop
their political consciousness, to organise their economic
struggle—this is our main and fundamental task.

So far, the Kisan Sabhas functioned only as organs for the
expression of spontaneous, unorganised peasant demands.
Now, for the first time, the Party gave the Sabhas an organised platform of demands. The abolition of *zamindars* and
taluqdars, and the cancellation of all peasant loans formed
the main demands. 'Abolish the *zamindari* system' became
such a strong demand, that Congress Ministries were forced
to take notice of the movement. Other supplementary demands
were voiced : halve all rents; abolish all rent for small holdings; enforce the punishment for *begar* (forced labour) by
zamindars; restrain the foreclosure of peasant homes, farm-
implements and land for non-payment of loans; organise co-
operative and collective farms. And thus, the kisan movement
struck deep roots in the countryside through its new-found
radicalism.

J.P. organised a huge Kisan Sabha Conference at Gaya.
Acharya Narendra Dev presided. Over 100,000 peasants and
farmers from all over the country attended the meeting. Later,
a meeting of Bihari Kisans was held at Vihpur, with J.P.
presiding. Bihar, at the time, had a Congress Ministry—J.P.,
at the head of the peasantry, started the Bakasht *satyagraha*
to press home their demands. The Bakasht movement in
Kheda became a celebrated turning point in the history of
peasant struggle in India. J.P. had played a prime role in
making it possible.

The offices of the Congress Socialist Party were situated in
Kabir Chaura in Benares. From its very inception, J.P. had
been General Secretary of the Party. The other office-bearers
had been : M.R. Masani, Mohanlal Gautam, N.G. Gore and
E.M.S. Namboodiripad.

The organisation of industrial workers proceeded apace, but
separately from the agricultural sector. At the time when the
C.S.P. was launched, there were three all-India working-class
organisations in existence—the Indian Trade Union Federation;

the All-India Trade Union Congress; and the Red Trade Union Congress. There was very little co-ordination between these bodies; they viewed each other as rivals, not as similar unions organised towards the same end. When the C.S.P. was born, it achieved the singular feat of fusing all three organisations into a single All-India Mazdoor Sangh. From then on, it worked to establish further unions wherever workers were not already organised.

Other Labour leaders also worked towards bringing about a fusion of the All-India Trade Union Congress and the National Trade Union Federation. Prominent among them were N.M. Joshi, Harihar Nath Shastri, R.S. Ruikar, V. Vishwanath and V.V. Giri.

Most of J.P.'s work for the Labour movement centred in Bihar. Hundreds of party workers went to jail, because of their strike-organising activities. Particularly in Jamshedpur, J.P. was responsible for laying a strong foundation for the trade unions in the iron industry. In 1940 when the workers of the Tar Company were on strike, J.P. went personally to Jamshedpur and mobilised the workers. A few days later, he was arrested for making inflammatory speeches and inciting the workers to stop work. He languished in jail for nine months.

J.P. brought out and published an English weekly called *Congress Socialist*, edited by Asoka Mehta with its offices at 139, Meadows Street, Fort, Bombay.

Clearly, the intention of the Party was to create a whole web of activities and organisations to further its purposes of propagating socialism. Apart from the Kisan and Mazdoor bodies and the above weekly, J.P. also gave his time to organising a Youth Society, a Women's Society, and a Self-Help Society as supplementary socialist bodies. J.P. drew up a list of five hundred books on Marxism, Trade Unionism, revolutionary philosophy, sociology and economics. Socialist book clubs were organised in a score of cities, so that members could have easy and inexpensive access to these books. Prominent left-wing political figures were invited to become foundation members of the club. A letter from Jayaprakash to Subhas Chandra Bose in this connection is preserved :

My dear Subhas Babu,

Sometime back I wrote to you about the Socialist Book Club which we wish to organise. I also sent you a copy of the memorandum and rules of the Club. We would like to know if you agree to be a foundation member of the Club and also a member of its advisory council.

The day I wrote to you I also cabled Jawaharlal for his consent to the foundation membership. I regret to say that he has declined our request because he says he does not know well what the scheme is like.

I shall be in Calcutta on the 25th and will stay for a few days to raise funds for the Club. We are counting on your active help in this.

With regards,
Yours affectionately,
Jayaprakash

The Party also organised a number of study camps. All young people and political workers were invited to participate in sessions of an itinerant political school. At each place, the speakers would halt for a month, and lecture on selected political and sociological topics. One such school opened in Bihar at Sonepur, and was known as the Political Summer School. Jayaprakash Narayan was one of the professors. So was Narendra Dev.

The second big study circle lasted from the 15th to 31st May (1937) at Almora (U.P.). Yusuf Meherally was the convener, and the meetings took place at Shail Ashram, about 8 miles away from Almora town, at the house of R.S. Pandit. Jawaharlal Nehru, Narendra Dev, Kamladevi, Sampurnanand, Dr. Lohia, Achyut Patwardhan, Asoka Mehta, Masani and Jayaprakash were among those present there.

In May-June 1939, the Kanyakubja College at Lucknow hosted a big socialist study camp. Nearly a hundred students and workers were given a thorough grounding in Marxism and the correct approach in solving the nation's problems.

In order to disseminate socialist ideas and the view-point of the party, Acharya Narendra Dev edited a Hindi weekly from Lucknow, *Sangharsh* (The Battle).

On the 23rd and 24th December 1936, The Faizpur session

of the Party, chaired by Jayaprakash Narayan, passed four resolutions. Satyavati Devi proposed that the King's Coronation be boycotted. Smt. Rajni Mukherjee's resolution was that India should decline to participate in any imperialist war. Mohanlal Kulkarni's resolution was : all political prisoners be released. And Dr. Ram Manohar Lohia proposed that in order to propagate the Party's views and principles, they should participate in the elections to the State Assemblies.

On the 12th and 13th April 1939, at the Lahore Party Session with Masani in the chair, the Congress Tricolour and the CSP red flag fluttered side by side. J.P. explained : 'There is no difference between the two flags, because their aims are the same : to strengthen the war of independence in the country. At first, admittedly, there were differences between the two, but now we accept the position that we must fight the Independence war under the Tricolour. It is grossly untrue that the socialists do not accept the Tricolour. We will fight for Independence under the Tricolour, and will spread socialist consciousness under our red flag.'

Two important resolutions were passed at the Lahore session : Achyut Patwardhan's support of the acts of the Congress Ministries, and endorsement of the fusing of the Trade Union Congress and National Trade Union Federation into one body, the All-India Trade Union Congress. The second was Dr. Lohia's resolution to utilise the international situation, particularly the imminence of the world war, for the benefit of the independence struggle.

On the 1st of September, 1939, World War II began with Germany's invasion of Poland. Important members of the Party happened to be in Patna on this day, and a hurried meeting in the Anjuman Islamia Hall was called. Acharya Narendra Dev presided. As the first speaker to address the assembled delegates, J.P. said :

This is an imperialist war. We will oppose it. Today, we announce this intention in this meeting. A time will come when we will not be allowed to hold a meeting, then on the streets, in by-lanes and if need be, from the roof tops, we will start our opposition to the war. We are going to take advantage of this war to win independence for ourselves.

Immediately afterwards, the Working Committee of the Party met at Lucknow, and in no uncertain terms, castigated the war as an 'imperialist' war, and announced that the Party would not participate in the war-effort at all. The next session of the Working Committee which met at Wardha drew up a concrete programme :

(1) To propagate opposition to the war by organising strikes ; (2) To convert the local Congress Committees to an anti-war posture; (3) To organise the Party workers to break the law and to organise a people's movement against the Government ordinances in Punjab and Bengal, where it had been made unlawful to agitate against the war; (4) To remove all restrictions on the activities of party-workers in those Provinces where Congress Ministries were in power; (5) To further the task of recruiting *swayamsevaks* (volunteers); (6) To go on with the other tasks of the Party, in particular, the organisation of workers and peasants.

A war committee was formed to see that these goals were fulfilled. At the same time, the Congress Working Committee was in session at Wardha, and J.P. was specially invited to attend.

After much deliberation, the Committee offered in September to support the British in their War against fascism provided that the British Government declared what their war aims were, and that they give an assurance that independence would be granted to India soon after the war, and that during the war Indians would be included in the Central Government to share responsibility and power. In his statement made on 17 October, 1939, the Viceroy explained nothing and gave no assurances to the Congress. The response of the Party was to condemn the Viceroy's statement and to call upon the Congress Ministries to resign. By the end of the month the Congress Governments in the provinces came to an end and Governor's rule began.

The C.S.P.'s stand against the 'imperialist war', however, soon met with unexpected opposition. Just before the war started in 1939, the Congress had a session at Tripuri, at which Subhas Chandra Bose was re-elected President. The C.S.P. could claim some credit for his victory, for it had backed him to the hilt against Dr. Pattabhi Sitaramayya. Gandhi, however, took Sitaramayya's defeat as a personal rebuke, and his supporters in the Working Committee resigned their seats. J.P. was understandably upset and tried to persuade Gandhi to retract this step and thrash out the issue on the floor of the committee. But tempers had flared on both sides, and Bose's faction was adamant that the Gandhian 'moderates' should leave the Congress. A split seemed imminent. The C.S.P. had always maintained that the Congress, with the many shades of political interest it represented, should pull together. J.P. tried hard to effect a rapprochement, and dissociated himself from the belligerents.

The next session at Calcutta saw the breach widen. Not placated by the redistribution of offices within the Congress, Bose's supporters withdrew from the Party altogether, and formed the Forward Bloc as a separate, parallel organisation. Not the clash of armies in Europe, but the schism within its ranks now claimed the attention of the Congressmen. Jayaprakash Narayan sent a letter to the Ramgarh Congress in which he counselled unity to face the enormity of the tasks ahead.

At the time when the Congress Socialist Party came into being, four other political groups claiming to be *socialist* were already in existence ; the Communists, the M.N. Roy group, the Punjab Socialist Party, and the Bengal Labour Party. Jayaprakash Narayan, Narendra Dev and their associates were in favour of creating a broad socialist front to fight imperialism. In particular, J.P. wanted to win over the Communists towards his views, and to work together. In January, 1936, at the Meerut session of the C.S.P., the Party proclaimed itself as a Marxist party, and invited the Bolsheviks to join its ranks.

The Bolsheviks had been hostile to the C.S.P. from the very beginning, and refused to acknowledge that it represented a Marxist or socialist party at all. The C.S.P., they maintained, was a leftist fringe of 'bourgeois reformists' and camp-followers of Gandhi.

However, because of the rise of the fascism in Europe, the Communist International had called for a coalescence of bourgeois democrats, revisionist socialists and the 'genuine' Marxist parties. The Communist Party of India was rebuked for standing apart from the national movement. In response to criticism, the Indian Bolsheviks began to talk about a National Democratic Front to fight imperialism. Soon after, members of the Communist Party began to trickle into the C.S.P. Namboodiripad, A.K. Gopalan, P. Sundarayya, Ramamurthy, Z. Ahmed, Batlivala and many others became members. Four of them were immediately co-opted to the Working Committee of the C.S.P.

It was not an easy relationship. The suspicion that the Communists would try and gain control of the C.S.P. remained a constant source of tension. Outside the councils of the Party, members of the C.P.I. sneeringly referred to it as a "bourgeois" appendage. Understandably, there was considerable unease while the coalition lasted, and at one point, Masani, Achyut Patwardhan, Dr. Lohia and Asoka Mehta threatened to resign.

A well-known clash occurred in 1938, at the Lahore session of the C.S.P. The Communists promulgated a thesis, 'Leftist Unity', which would have compromised the relationship of the C.S.P. with the Congress. Narendra Dev, Achyut Patwardhan, Asoka Mehta and Kamladevi countered it with a thesis of their own, maintaining that the original programme and outlook of the C.S.P. still held true, and did not need changing. This view was upheld by the delegates present. Another trial of strength ensued when a new working committee had to be elected. Again the communists suffered a setback when the C.S.P. incumbents were returned with large majorities. The session culminated in an uproar when Masani disclosed possession of an intercepted letter which was a blueprint for a communist take-over of the C.S.P.

At first J.P. continued to strive for understanding between the partners. Ultimately, however, threatened with the withdrawal of Masani, Patwardhan, Lohia, and Kamladevi from the Party, he admitted that the alliance had not worked well.

With the onset of the war, the attitude of the C.P.I. hardened into opposition. It labelled the C.S.P. a "counter-revolutionary" party, Subhas Bose's Forward Bloc and the Congress were castigated as lackeys of the British imperialism.

Now there was no further room for negotiations. At the Ramgarh session in 1940, the communists were unanimously expelled from the C.S.P. In 1941, Purushottam Trikamdas, General Secretary of the C.S.P., wrote this epitaph on the alliance : 'We are not sorry that the experiment was made; but because of the harrowing experience we have to pass through, we are not sorry it has ended. . . . It was a bad dream, a nightmare; let us forget it and get on with the task.'

The Royists, too, were no longer with the C.S.P. M.N. Roy had returned from Soviet Russia in 1931, and took his supporters from the C.P.I. with him to form the Roy Group. Almost immediately afterwards, Roy was arrested by the Government, and was in jail when the C.S.P. was launched. In 1936, when he was released, Roy was sympathetic towards the C.S.P., and talked of joining it. Gradually, however, he became critical of the separateness of the C.S.P. *within* the Congress. Then came the Assembly elections, and the C.S.P. opposed the setting up of the Congress Ministries in the Provinces. Roy supported the Congress move, and broke completely with the C.S.P. Jayaprakash Narayan wrote : 'Perhaps he had come to realise that the Congress Socialist Party could not be a plaything in his hands, nor a platform that he could use to boost his own ego . . . .'

Later, at the Tripuri Congress, the Royists sided with Subhas Bose. Soon after, they broke completely with the Congress, and formed the Radical Party.

The Labour Party in Bengal, from the very beginning, had set its face against the C.S.P. J.P., however, was particularly keen on securing its cooperation. His persistence brought about a short honeymoon of the Bengal unit of the C.S.P. and the Labour Party, and a Joint Committee was set up. Soon after, however, the Labourites joined the C.P.I., then they left them to join the Forward Bloc and ultimately merged the Labour Party's identity with the Bengal Congress.

The C.S.P. was more successful in winning over the Punjab Socialist Party to its fold. The Punjab Socialists were a group of young firebrands—Sardar Bhagat Singh was one of them— who had started off in militant opposition to the Congress. Gradually, however, their ideological differences were worn away, and the Punjab Socialist group was absorbed into the C.S.P.

One other question merits discussion: the relationship of the C.S.P. with Subhas Chandra Bose's Forward Bloc.

Subhas Bose was convalescing in Europe at the time when the C.S.P. was formed. While still in Europe, he had published *Indian Struggle*, in which he had praised fascism as a means of mobilising the energies of a nation. By the time Bose returned to India, he had apparently changed his mind, and spoke glowingly of socialism. Jayaprakash Narayan succeeded in enlisting his support for the activities of the Party. At the Haripur Congress Session, where he was elected Chairman, Bose praised the Congress Socialist Party in no uncertain terms, and extended his help in publishing socialist literature and in organising the Book Club.

Then came the historic clash at the Tripuri Congress. The C.S.P. supported Subhas Chandra Bose against the Gandhian faction, and helped to elect him to the Chair. Sardar Patel and Rajendra Prasad resigned from the Working Committee, and a split in the Congress seemed imminent. At this point, J.P. stepped in as mediator, and the C.S.P. decided not to take sides in the struggle.

As the conflict dragged on and the scales tipped in favour of Gandhi, Subhas Bose resigned as Chairman, and Rajendra Prasad replaced him. No C.S.P. members were included in the newly constituted Working Committee.

Immediately afterwards, Subhas Bose withdrew with his following, and launched the Forward Bloc as a Party in opposition to the Congress. Nevertheless, despite the political differences that now separated Subhas Bose from the Congress, Jayaprakash Narayan did not lose his esteem for Bose as a great patriot and a great fighter for Indian independence.

A winter morning in 1940, Jayaprakash Narayan was sitting with his friend, Phoolan Prasad Varma, and sipping hot tea. A friend interrupted them with the news that he (J.P.) had been served with a warrant of arrest. He had been charged with making an unlawful speech on the 18th of February that year at Jamshedpur. Two days later, Jayaprakash was put behind bars in the Chaivasa Jail. Gandhi, Nehru and the editorials in the *Searchlight* and *Indian Nation* immediately protested against this flagrant repressive measure. Gandhi wrote 'The arrest of Sri Jayaprakash Narayan is unfortunate. He is no ordinary worker. He is an authority on socialism. It may be said that what he does not know of Western socialism no body else in India does. He is a fine fighter. He has forsaken all for the sake of the deliverance of his country. His industry is tireless. His capacity for suffering is not to be excelled . . . .'

Nine months later, J.P. was removed from Chaivasa to the Hazaribagh Jail, where he joined the political detenus of the Communist Party and the Forward Bloc. Instead of comradeship he was treated with hostility. Many of these fellow-prisoners did not talk to him at all. The reason was pure pique—J.P. was a friend of Nehru and Gandhi; yet it was impossible to identify him as a right-winger or reactionary. How could one deal with such a man ?

In the jail, J.P.'s political work continued uninterrupted. To those who were willing to listen, he talked endlessly about politics and political economy. Gradually, he established contact with associates whose activities had not been curtailed by imprisonment. Soon, by smuggling out despatches, he somehow managed to write articles in the *Searchlight, National Herald* and *Bombay Chronicle*. They were signed, simply, 'A Congress Socialist'.

While he was still in jail, Germany surged across the Maginot Line and invaded France. Soon afterwards the Congress made a pact with the British, and agreed to form a National Government. J.P. penned a draft resolution to Gandhi, asking him, (if he accepted his assessment of the political situation) to place it before the Working Committee at Ramgarh. The resolution read:

The Congress and the country are on the eve of a great national upheaval. The final battle for freedom is soon to be fought. This will happen when the whole world is being shaken by mighty forces of change. Out of the catastrophe of the European War, thoughtful minds everywhere are anxious to create a new world—a world based on the co-operative goodwill of nations and men. At such a time the Congress considers it necessary to state definitely the ideals of freedom for which it stands and for which it is soon to invite the Indian people to undergo the utmost suffering.

The free Indian Nation shall work for peace between nations and total rejection of armaments and for the method of peaceful settlement of national disputes, through some international authority freely established. It will endeavour particularly to live on the friendliest terms with its neighbours, whether they be great powers or small nations, and shall covet no foreign territory.

The law of the land will be based on the will of the people freely expressed by them. The ultimate basis of maintenance of order shall be the sanction and concurrence of the people.

Free India shall guarantee full individual and civil liberty and cultural and religious freedom provided that there shall be no freedom to overthrow by violence the constitution framed by the Indian people through a Constituent Assembly.

The State shall not discriminate in any manner between citizens of the nation. Every citizen shall be guaranteed equal rights. All distinction of birth and privilege shall be abolished. There shall be no titles emanating either from inheritance, birth or social status.

The political and economic organisation of the State shall be based on principles of social justice and economic freedom. While the organisation shall work towards the satisfaction of the national requirements of every member of Society, material satisfaction shall not be its sole objective. It shall aim at healthy living and the moral and intellectual development of the individual. To this end and to secure social justice, the state shall endeavour to promote small-scale production carried on by individual or co-operative effort for the equal benefit of all concerned. All large scale collective production shall be eventually brought under collective ownership and control and in this behalf the state shall begin by nationalising heavy transport, shipping, mining and the heavy industries. The textile industry shall be progressively decentralised.

The life of the villages shall be reorganised and the villages shall be made self-governing units, self-sufficient in as large a measure as possible. The land laws of the country shall be drastically revised on the principle that land shall belong to the actual cultivator alone, and that no cultivator shall have more land than is necessary to support his family on a fair standard of living. This will end the various systems of landlordism on the one hand and farm bondage on the other.

The State shall protect the interests of the propertied classes but when these impinge upon the interests of those who have been poor and down-trodden, it shall defend the latter and thus restore the balance of social justice.

In all State-owned and State-managed enterprises, the workers shall be represented in the management through their elected representatives and shall have an equal share in it with the representatives of the Government.

In the Indian States, there shall be complete democratic Government established and in accordance of social distinction and equality between citizens, there shall not be any titular head of the States in the persons of Rajahs and Nawabs.

Gandhi commented on the letter thus :

I liked it and read his letter and the draft to the Working Committee. The Committee, however, thought that the idea of having only one resolution for the Ramgarh Congress should be strictly adhered to, and that the original as framed at Patna, should not be tampered with. The reasoning of the Committee was unexceptional and the draft resolution was dropped without any discussion of its merits. I informed Jayaprakash of the result of my effort. He wrote back suggesting that he would be satisfied if I could do the next best thing, namely publish it with full concurrence of such as I could give.

I have no difficulty in complying with Shri Jayaprakash's wishes. As an ideal to be reduced to practice as soon as possible after India comes into her own, I endorse in general all except one of the propositions enunciated by Shri Jayaprakash.

I have claimed that I was a socialist long before anyone I know in India had avowed their need. But my socialism was natural to me and not adopted from any books. It came out of my unshakeable belief in non-violence. No

man could be actively non-violent and not rise against
social injustice no matter where it occurred. Unfortunately
Western socialists have, so far as I know, believed in the
necessity of violence for enforcing socialist doctrines.

After a few months, J.P. was released and he resolved not to
allow himself to be imprisoned again. This meant living and
working in hiding, with the utmost secrecy. It did not mean
abandoning his political mission or curtailing his activity.

Immediately after, he contacted Gandhi, and then Subhas
Chandra Bose, still intent on bringing about a rapprochement
between the two, but his talks with Bose were unfruitful.
From Calcutta, J.P. went to Bihar to bolster the peasant movement (led by Swami Sahajanand) in its struggle against the
repressive machinery of the State.

From Bihar he travelled to Gujarat and then to Bombay,
where he attended meetings and met other leaders—all this,
in disguise. And then suddenly, he was re-arrested and sent to
the Arthur Road Prison in Bombay city, and from there, to
Deoli Camp, where he joined about five hundred prisoners
under political detention. Once again, J.P. utilised this period
of enforced 'rest' in busying himself in the only kind of political activity open to him : in gaol, he organised political discussion groups and debates which forced all the participants
to sharpen their views and reflect on the tense situation in the
country. When he could, he read avidly, a luxury which was
often difficult to indulge in when he was free and fervently
active. But it was not enough that he could surround himself
with news and views of politics and, therefore, began to look
for a way of establishing contact with his associates who were
still free. His first attempt at smuggling a letter out of jail
failed and succeeded at the same time.

Prabhavati came to visit J.P. one day, and was not quick
enough to perceive that he wanted to hand over a packet of
letters to her. The guard, who detected the move, seized the
packet and reported the incident to the Camp Superintendent,
who ordered that no visitors be allowed to see J.P. for three
months.

A few days later, however, the contents of one of the letters
from the confiscated packet appeared in the newspapers.

Apparently, the Government felt that J.P.'s views, if published, would alienate him from Gandhi and the Congress.

Gandhi's attitude however, was not one of anger. He wrote :

I know that Jayaprakash does not agree with my non-violent principles, but he is not to blame for that. He spent many years in America, and was educated there. It is natural that his thinking be influenced by the doctrines of foreign movements. But one thing is clear : whatever he has done has been completely in the cause of national freedom. Whatever our disagreements and differences, I have not for a moment doubted his courage, sacrifice and strength of purpose. I do not think a foreign power, that has ruled India for an age through force and violence, has the right to accuse Jayaprakash of believing in violence. By publishing his letter, the Government has tried to bring him into disrepute. If they think Jayaprakash is guilty of believing in violence, then the foremost offender is the Government itself. The English power was established in India through the bloody exploits of Clive and Hastings, and it has been maintained by the same methods. They are the primary criminals, and before anyone else they are the ones who should be hanged.

Understandably, it was not enough that his voice be heard above the din of activity and war. J.P. longed to escape and to be actively associated with all that was happening in the political world outside. And if escape from Deoli Camp was not physically possible, then he would create a furore by going on a hunger strike. Together with about two hundred and fifty prisoners, J.P. began fasting. There was an immediate response from all over the country. Nationalist students in Kanpur, Gauhati, Bombay, Karachi, and elsewhere marched in procession to protest against the detention of the prisoners. Questions were raised in the Provincial Assemblies. And ultimately the inmates of Deoli Camp were despatched to jails in their own provinces—J.P. went back to the Hazari-bagh Jail.

Before he left—weak and exhausted by the fast—he wrote to Jawaharlal Nehru enquiring about Narendra Dev's health. It was typical that in the midst of his own troubles, he could

reach out and encompass the discomfiture of a friend. The
fragments of the letter that escaped the censor's scissors
read :

Deoli Detention Camp
Deoli, Rajputana
December 7, 1941

My dear Bhai,

*Warmest greetings to you . . . (censored)... I cannot but feel
extremely happy at your being out when the country needs your
guidance most . . . (censored) . . . you must have heard about
Narendra Dev's health. One of his greatest failings is that he
cannot take care of himself. And I am afraid he will become a
permanent invalid unless he is promptly looked after. What he
needs most is not medicines but a long rest in a suitable place.
No place in the U.P. or anywhere in the north will suit him.
Some districts of Maharashtra such as Satara, or places further south—Ballary, Anantpur—might be good for him—even
Gujarat might suit him. Left to himself, I am certain, he would
vegetate somewhere in the U.P., or at the best Sri Prakash
might take him to Benares to his Sevashram. What we call
SANKOCH will prevent him from asking any of his
innumerable friends to do anything for him. I am therefore
writing to you to take a particular interest in this matter and
to pack him off to some suitable place. You must not leave this
thing to his option. In this matter you must treat him as one
treats a child. You may consult Bapu also in this connection as
he has been taking keen interest in Narendra Dev's health.*

*I am well now and am slowly regaining my strength. Sethji too
is well and sends you his greetings. Gautam is down with
Malaria and is in the hospital. Other friends are well.*

With love,
Yours,
Jayaprakash

He was also still preoccupied with the split in the Congress,
and did not let up in his efforts for conciliation with Subhas
Chandra Bose. A letter which he wrote to Subhas Bose just
before he left the jail is available :

Subhas Babu,

*I have to say some important things to you. The Communist
Party attacks the Forward Bloc and the Congress Socialist*

Party. And we persist in our disunity. Why did we allow Mr.
Ranga to join the Communists ? Why don't our members keep
in contact with Kavishwar, Kamath, etc. in order to strengthen
their association with our parties ? Do you recall what I said to
you when I was out of jail—why don't we act in this scheme
for the good of the country ? We do not have a duty to stay in
bondage. We have always been opposed to the World War, and
want to utilise this situation for a war of National independence.

The Hazaribagh Jail is situated in rocky, forested terrain. The
dour buildings had been constructed during the first World
War to house the State prisoners, and its wards were filled
with Bengali terrorists, and members of the Ghadar Party from
the Punjab. Each ward had between 26 and 28 cells, and
there was also the Magistry Cell, where 'hard labour' was
meted out through stints at the *chakki* (grinding stone). One
single instance of a jail-break was on record, and the man
who had escaped, Sucha Singh, had been re-arrested and was
back in prison when Jayaprakash Narayan arrived.

Meanwhile, the political scene was simmering. The Congress distrust of the British increased, and it became convinced
that the British 'had no intention to recognise India's independence, and would, if they could, continue to hold this
country indefinitely in bondage for British exploitation'. Then,
in October 1940, Gandhi launched the individual civil disobedience movement. Nearly 30,000 Congressmen courted
imprisonment during the years 1940-41.

By 1942, the war had moved to India's doorstep. In
February that year Singapore fell to the Japanese, and Rangoon a month later. Churchill and Roosevelt turned their
attention to the eastern theatre of war. The (Congress) prisoners were released soon after the bombing of Pearl Harbour.
Now, the fall of Rangoon prompted Churchill to despatch to
India in March 1942, a British Cabinet Minister, Sir Stafford
Cripps. The Indian political deadlock had suddenly become a
matter of grave concern not only to the British, but to their
allies, the U.S.A. and China, and they pressed for a solution
to the internal conflict.

The Cripps Mission had aroused hopes in the Congress
circles and suspicion among the Muslim Leaguers, but turned

out to be disappointing to the former and stimulating to the latter. The failure of the Mission further sharpened the Congress hostility towards the British. The approach of Japan to India's eastern frontier aroused among the Congressmen mixed feelings of hope and fear.

There was the fear that Japan might turn out to be a new imperialist. Nehru's anti-British attitude was not, therefore, a plea to submit to Japan. He wrote to President Roosevelt :

Though the way of our choice may be closed to us, and we are unable to associate ourselves with the activities of the British authorities in India, still we shall do our utmost not to submit to the Japanese or any other aggression and invasion. We, who have struggled for so long for freedom and against an old aggression, would prefer to perish rather than submit to a new invader.

Underneath the fear was the hope that Japan might liberate India. Subhas Chandra Bose, who had escaped from British India to Germany (Berlin) in January 1941, had formed the provisional Government of Free India with the support of the Axis powers. In 1942, he was assuring Indians from the Azad Hind Radio, Germany, that Japan was 'our ally, our helper. Co-operate with the Japanese in order to eliminate British domination and establish a new order.'

The Congress now looked for guidance to Gandhi, who was in a more uncompromising mood than ever. He decided that Britain must *quit India* immediately. 'There are powerful elements of fascism in British rule, and in India these are the elements which we see and feel every day. If the British wish to document their right to win the war and make the world better, they must purify themselves by surrendering power in India.'

Immediately after, the Congress Working Committee passed a resolution on the 6th July, 1942 asking the British to withdraw from India, threatening a civil disobedience movement if they remained. The resolution was endorsed by the All-India Congress Committee on the 8th August, 1942 at Bombay. The very next day all members of the Congress Working Committee and Mahatma Gandhi were arrested and the Indian National Congress was outlawed. Gandhi reiterated his call for non-violent agitation, but his mood

had changed, and it was not clear that he would condemn
the nation for choosing whatever method it found suitable
to force the British to *quit*. Gandhi had sounded the clarion-
call—'Do or Die' :

> You may take it from me that I am not going to strike
> a bargain with the viceroy for Ministries and the like. I
> am not going to be satisfied with anything short of comp-
> lete freedom. Maybe, he will propose the abolition of
> salt tax, the drink evil, etc. But I will say—'Nothing less
> than freedom.'

> Here is a *mantra*, a short one, that I give you. You
> may . . . on your hearts and let every breath of yours give
> expression to it. The *mantra* is 'Do or Die'. We shall
> either free India or die in the attempt, we shall not live
> to see the perpetuation of our slavery. Every true Cong-
> ressman or woman will join the struggle with an inflexi-
> ble determination not to remain alive to see the country
> in bondage and slavery. Let that be your pledge. Keep
> jails out of your consideration. If the Government keep me
> free, I will spare you the trouble of filling the jails . . . .

> . . . take a pledge, with God and your own conscience
> as witness, that you will no longer rest till freedom is
> achieved and will be prepared to lay down your lives in
> the attempt to achieve it.

> . . . Nothing, however, should be done secretly. This
> is an open rebellion. In this struggle secrecy is a sin. A
> free man would not engage in a secret movement. It is
> likely that you gain freedom, you have a C.I.D. of your
> own, in spite of my advice to the contrary. But in the
> present struggle, we have to work openly and to receive
> bullets on our chest, without taking to our heels . . . .

Hundreds of thousands of people responded to Gandhi's
call passionately. Finding no Congress leaders outside prison
to guide them, they resorted to violence. Trains were derailed
and looted, police stations were set ablaze and telegraph
lines cut. Particularly in Bihar and U.P., the apparatus of
the British Government ground to a complete halt, and the
army was called in.

With all the Congress leaders behind bars, the Socialists

assumed the task of masterminding the movement and
directing the rampaging crowds. Every day there were re-
ports of police firings and fresh arrests. Achyut Patwardhan, Dr. Lohia and their companions formed a Central Mobilisation Committee. At the best of times, however, they were
little-known substitutes for the Congress stalwarts.

All this time, Jayaprakash Narayan was pacing his cell in
rage and frustration. At the high-tide of the movement, he
found himself chained and confined, unable to play any role
at all. He decided to attempt a jail-break, and explained
his plans to the other inmates. The very next day, the guards
were changed and the security arrangements were intensified.
Somehow, the plan had leaked to the authorities, and it now
seemed a more difficult project than ever.

J.P. was determined, however, to break away, whatever
the odds. He sketched out a new scheme, and this time con-
fided only in a select group of people he could trust in. And
they waited for an opportunity.

August and September (1942) came and went. Many
prisoners were tried, sentenced and despatched to jails in
other parts of the country. As the number of prisoners in
the jail dwindled, the armed guards were removed.

The prisoners in the 'A' class cells received a daily food
ration worth 10 annas (62 paise). Jayaprakash Narayan
together with a group of satyagrahis, however, protested
against the treatment meted out to the prisoners in the 'C'
class cells, and opted to live in similar conditions until
conditions were ameliorated. On the inferior diet which this
entailed, J.P.'s health declined steadily, and his legs were
afflicted with sciatica. Through all these difficulties, the
plan of escape kept turning over in his mind.

Every evening, before the prisoners were locked up in
separate cells, a sergeant-at-arms conducted a roll call. Even
if J.P. managed to scale the walls a couple of hours before
this, it would not take long for the guards to catch up with
him, for he could not walk fast. One solution was to wait
for a festival day, when the roll was called late, and the
wards were left open till midnight.

Yogendra Shukla, a tried and trusted Bihari revolutionary,
went over the plan carefully with J.P. They could take with

them only a limited number of people. Only this had to be
borne in mind: of those who escaped only the most active
and politically indispensable leaders would be selected.
Personal considerations were brushed aside. They also had
to arrange matters so that a few appointed friends would
undertake to divert the attention of the guards and wardens
while the group scaled the walls. The men selected to escape
with Jayaprakash Narayan and Shukla were : Surya Narain
Singh, Gulabchand, Ram Nandan Mishra, and as guide,
Shaligram of the Hazaribagh Congress Committee—six persons in all. Only twelve persons knew of the plan.

On Diwali morning, the inmates set about preparing
for festival. Sweets were prepared, the inmates played
badminton and cards, and sang *bhajans*. As evening approached, 42 *diyas* were lit to commemorate the events of that
year, and the inmates toured the wards in procession, singing
and cheering. With the festivities in full swing, the six men
slipped away under cover of darkness, and scaled the wall
with the help of dhotis knotted together as a rope.

Their absence was not detected until the next morning.
Those of the inmates who were in the know dropped the
mosquito-nets over the beds of the six escapees, and pre-
tended as if they were unwell. Early in the morning, however, the prison sirens began wailing, and the prisoners
awoke in a flurry to the news that the men had gone.

All night the six men walked and ran through scrub jungle
and wet, slushy ground. Most of them were barefoot and
inadequately protected against the cold.

As day broke, the men had to be more careful about
being spotted. By afternoon, they had all to draw upon
special reserves of strength to keep on going on for they had
eaten nothing at all. Jayaprakash Narayan, the weakest of
them all, because of the pain in his legs, hobbled along
supporting himself on the shoulders of his comrades.

A little later they noticed a plane circling overhead. Perhaps, the Ranchi airfield had been alerted about the escape,
and they were reconnoitring the area from the air. The
men decided to proceed separately so as not to attract
attention. Yogendra Shukla and Shaligram joined hands and
made a cradle for J.P. to sit on, and in this strange way, they

all proceeded.

At night they met a man with a bullock-cart going in the same direction. They told him that they were travellers who had been robbed on the way, but he would not believe the story and allow them to ride with him.

At midnight they stopped and snatched four hours of sleep, and then, somehow, carried on walking. The next afternoon, they slipped into Shaligram's village, where they ate their first square meal after 35 hours. Shaligram got hold of a bullock cart; J.P., Ram Nandan and Gulab Chand, disguised as peasants got onto the cart. Yogendra, Shaligram and Suraj, wearing rustic turbans and carrying axes, so as to look like woodcutters, walked behind. On the way they came across a police checkpost, but their disguises served them well, and no suspicion was aroused.

At length they reached Gaya, where they arranged to have the bullock-cart returned. They split up into two parties: Jayaprakash Narayan, Shaligram and Ram Nandan decided to go to Benares. Shuklaji, Suraj and Gulab Chand left for Gangapur in North Bihar.

By this time, the news of the sensational escape had spread all over the country. As further insurance against being recognised, the six men donned new disguises. Some of them shaved their heads and wore the sacred thread to look like devout *pandas*. Others wore Muslim dress and talked from deep in their throats.

From Gaya, J.P. and the other two borrowed another bullock-cart and forded the river Phalgu by night. Then on through Godaru, Obra, Pamarganj, where they left the cart behind, and got onto a ferry on the river Sone. Seven miles down-stream, avoiding a checkpoint, they crossed the river, and entered Shahabad district. Here J.P. was on his home territory at last, where if his strange appearance aroused suspicion, his fluent Bhojpuri would still all doubts that he was a villager.

The next day, the three of them boarded a passenger train at Karbadiya station up to Mughalsarai. Shaligram left Mughalsarai for Benares alone, in order to make arrangements to keep Jayaprakashji and Ram Nandan under cover. Shaligram, however, was recognised as soon as he arrived.

His only course was to leave Banaras and continue in hiding.

Jayaprakashji and Ram Nandan left for Banaras by *ekka* the next day. They crossed the river separately by ferry, and landed at Nagva Ghat near the university. They learnt that the Government had announced a reward of five thousand rupees for J.P.'s capture.

Jayaprakash Narayan quickly established contact with the men who were at the helm of affairs during the August movement in northern India—Vishvanath Mishra, Shreeram Sharma, Mohanlal Gautam. Banaras was the storm-centre of the movement in this part of the country.

A brief look around him to get acquainted with recent developments convinced him that Banaras was not the place to be in. Wearing European clothes, and sporting a beard, Jayaprakashji left for Bombay.

Here he found that his friends and associates were already working tirelessly to give the movement shape and coherence. Achyut Patwardhan, Yugal Kishor, Dr. Keskar, Divakar, Aruna Asaf Ali, Sucheta Kripalani, Yusuf Meherally and many others had filled in positions of leadership vacated by the imprisoned Congress leaders.

The British unleashed a brutal repression to quell the movement. Everything had to be organised in secrecy. Emissaries were despatched all over the country to coordinate the activities of nationalist bodies. The Congress and C.S.P. periodicals and bulletins, which were banned, continued to appear from hidden hand-presses, and were circulated widely.

Jayaprakash Narayan jumped into the fray. After studying the situation, he penned in January, 1943 the first of his historic letters, 'To all Fighters for Freedom' :

Revolutionary Greetings !
Comrades,

   Let me first of all offer you and all those who have been made prisoners of war my heartiest congratulations on the magnificent battle already given to the enemy. Nothing like it ever happened or was expected to happen in this our long-suffering and suppressed country. It truly was the 'Open Rebellion' envisaged by our incomparable leader, Mahatma Gandhi.

   The Rebellion, no doubt, seems to have been suppressed for the moment. But I hope you will agree with me that it has been suppressed only for the moment. This should cause us no surprise. As a matter of fact, had the very first assault been successful and had it completely crushed imperialism, that in reality would have been a matter of surprise. The very fact that the enemy himself has admitted that the Rebellion came pretty near destroying his power, shows how successful was the first phase of our National Revolution.

And how was the first phase suppressed ? Was it the military power of the enemy, his unmitigated reign of goondaism, looting, arson and murder that did the job ? No. It is wrong to consider the 'Revolt' as having been 'suppressed'. The history of all Revolutions shows that a Revolution is not an event. It is a phase, a social process. And during the evolution of a revolution, tides and ebbs are normal. Our Revolution is at present going through the period of low water. This has come about, not because the superior physical force of the imperialist aggressors intervened, but because of two important reasons.

Firstly, there was no efficient organisation of the national revolutionary forces that could function and give effective lead to the mighty forces that were released. The Congress, though a great organisation, was not tuned to the pitch to which the revolution was to rise. The lack of organisation was so considerable that even important Congressmen were not aware of the progress of the revolt, and till late in the course of the Rising it remained a matter of debate in accordance with the Congress programme. The earnestness, the urgency, the determination that marked the attitude of leaders like Mahatma Gandhi, Dr. Rajendra Prasad or Sardar Patel failed to reflect in the hearts and minds of all Congress leaders.

Secondly, after the first phase of the Rising, there was no further programme placed before the people. After they had completely destroyed the British Raj in their areas, the people considered their tasks fulfilled, and went back to their homes not knowing what more to do. Nor was it their fault. The failure was ours; we should have supplied them with a programme for the next phase. When this was not done, the Revolt came to a standstill and the phase of the ebb began . . . .

What programme should have been placed before the people in the second phase ? The answer is suggested by the nature of revolutions. A revolution is not only a destructive process, it is at the same time a great constructive force. No revolution could succeed if it only destroyed . . . . Our Revolution too, having accomplished over large areas of the country the negative task of destruction, called for a positive programme. The people should have set up in their areas their own units of Revolutionary Government and created their own police and militia . . . .

The lack of efficient organisation and of a complete programme of National Revolution : these were two causes of the downward course of the first phase of the present Revolution.

The question now is : what are our present tasks ? First, to banish all depression from our minds and those of the people and create an atmosphere of joy instead at the success achieved and of hope for success in the future.

Second, we must keep steadfastly before our minds and of the people the nature of this Revolution. It is our last fight for freedom. Our objective can, therefore, be nothing but victory. There can be no half-way houses. The efforts that men like Rajagopalachari are making for the establishment of National Government are not only fruitless but positively harmful inasmuch as they distract public attention from the real issues. There is no compromise between the slogans of 'Quit India' and of 'National Government'. Those who are running after the slogan of Congress-League unity are merely serving the ends of imperialist propaganda. It is not the lack of unity that is obstructing the formation of a National Government, but the natural unwillingness of imperialism to liquidate itself. Mr. Churchill left no manner of doubt about it when he declared recently that he had not assumed the office of the King's first minister to preside over the liquidation of the Empire. He would be a foolish student of society indeed who expected empires to wither away of their own accord.

It is not the unity of all the important elements in Indian life, to quote the imperialist jargon, that is the need of the hour but the unity of all the national revolutionary forces. And these are already united under the flag of the Congress. Unity between the League and the Congress does not foreshadow the growth of these forces, but their absolute relation, for the

League cannot conceivably tread the path of revolution and freedom . . . .

The complete overthrow of imperialism, then is our objective and we must keep this steadfastly in view. There can be no compromise on this issue. Either we win or we lose. And lose we shall not . . . . Do not believe that the formal results of this war settled laboriously at the Peace Conference would settle the fate of the post-war world. War is a strange alchemist, and in its hidden chambers are such forces and powers brewed and distilled that they tear down the plans of the victorious and vanquished alike. No peace conference at the end of the last war decided that four mighty Empires of Europe and Asia should fall into dust—the Russian, the German, the Austrian and the Ottoman. Nor was the Russian, the German, the Turkish revolution decreed by Lloyd George, Clemenceau or Wilson.

Throughout the world where men are fighting, dying and suffering today, the alchemist is at work, just as he is in India, where he has already let loose a mighty social upheaval. Neither Churchill nor Roosevelt, neither Hitler nor Tojo will determine the fate of the world at the end of this war. It is force such as we represent that will fulfil that historic task. Can we doubt that revolutionary forces are stirring everywhere ? Can we believe that millions of people are undergoing unutterable sufferings without a thought for the future ? Can we believe that millions are satisfied with the lies that their rulers daily feed them with ? No, it cannot be so.

Having therefore definitely fixed our vision on the goal of total victory, we have to march ahead. What concretely must we do ? What does a general do when he loses or wins a battle ? He consolidates and prepares for the next battle . . . . Ours was not even a defeat. We really won the first round of the fight inasmuch as over large territories of the country the civil rule of the British aggressor was completely uprooted. The masses have now learnt from experience that the imposing edifice of the police and magistracy and law courts and prisons which goes by the name of British Raj is but a house of cards when they hurl against either collective power. This lesson is not likely to be forgotten and it constitutes the starting point for the next offensive.

Our third and most important task then at the present moment is to prepare for the next major offensive. Preparation, organisation, discipline—these are our present watchwords . . . .

With full confidence in the people and devotion to the cause, let us, then, march ahead. Let our steps be firm, our hearts resolute and our vision undimmed. The sun of the Indian freedom has already risen above the horizon. Let not the clouds of our own doubts and disputes, inaction and faithlessness, obscure the sun and drown us in our self-created darkness . . . .

Somewhere in India
Jayaprakash Narayan

As Jayaprakash Narayan emerged at the forefront of the political struggle, the Government intensified its efforts to recapture him. A warrant was issued :

'Jayaprakash Narayan and five other prisoners have escaped from Hazaribagh Central Jail. Anyone who captures them or furnishes information leading to their arrest will be given a reward of up to Rs. 21,000 (twenty-one thousand rupees) : Rs. 5,000 for Jayaprakash Narayan, Rs. 5,000 for Yogendra Shukla, Rs. 5,000 for Ram Nandan Mishra, Rs. 2,000 for Suraj Narayan Singh, Rs. 2,000 for Gulab Chand Gupta, alias Gulali, and Rs. 2,000 for Shaligram.'

Ramvriksh Benipuri has recalled the thrill which ran through the nation at J.P.'s escape. In a letter to a friend at the time, he wrote :

Dear friend,

You cannot imagine what Jayaprakash's escape means to us. We had lost, and we were not a little tired in mind and body. For some time our ardour had cooled, our energy had flagged. Because of repression, most people were plain scared. They looked upon us as saviours. They wanted to help, but in the daytime they did not want to see us at all. In August, they had uprooted the Government on their own. When the Government was re-established and retaliated, the people carried on in the hope that Subhas Babu's army would march in. We received messages that at any moment, an army of liberation would arrive. At night, we mistook every star for one of Subhas

Babu's planes. And slowly, people began to lose hope, and they resigned themselves to defeat. Then suddenly, we heard of Jayaprakash's escape, and the gloom lifted immediately. Our workers once again came to life, the spark was rekindled. The people began to believe that the Government could not keep our leaders in jail. Jayaprakash has broken out of jail, now we will break down the other jails and free Gandhi and the others. The people are fired with a strange courage. Now we will not rest till we win. 'Four hundred million cannot submit.'

Do or Die

To a political movement that had been shorn of its most eminent leaders Jayaprakash Narayan's escape was a tonic. Now once again, there was confidence that the energies of the people would not be expended in spontaneous, random acts, but would be guided towards a clear objective.

Six months after his jail-break, J.P. wrote the second of his letters entitled 'To All Fighters for Freedom'. It appeared on the 1st September, 1943. It read as follows :

. . . . For some months past, particularly since the correspondence between Gandhiji and the Viceroy was published, a controversy has sprung up among fighters on the question of violence and non-violence . . . . To me a controversy on this issue at this stage seems meaningless. Every fighter for freedom is free to choose his own method. Those who believe in similar methods should work together as a disciplined group . . . . Where 'Do or Die' is the mantra of action, there is no room for recrimination whatever. Those who believe in non-violence may harbour the fear that those who practise violence may compromise the position of Gandhiji. That fear is unfounded. Gandhiji's adherence to non-violence is so complete, his position in respect to it so clear, that not a hundred thousand Churchills and Amerys will be able to compromise him. Also, we must remember, that whatever we do, however we try, we can never prevent British statesmen, whether Tory or Labour, from telling lies, for lies are one of the central pillars of the Empire. Remember also that if there is violence in India no one but the British Government itself is responsible for it.

Another controversy that has been started since the publication of the Gandhi-Viceroy correspondence is whether the present struggle was started by the Congress and whether it can be called a Congress movement. It has been claimed by some, who have gone so far as to suggest that a rump A.I.C.C. should meet to withdraw the Bombay Resolution, that since Gandhi and other Congress leaders were arrested before they could make a formal declaration of war, this struggle is not a Congress struggle at all. According to the logic of this argument, no struggle, if the British were to arrest the leaders in time, could ever have the formal authority and sanction of the Congress. What is it that those who deny the authority of the Congress to the struggle would desire to have happened on the 9th of August (1942) after the cowardly attack on our leaders ? What do they think was the desire of Mahatma Gandhi and the Working Committee in the event of their arrest ? Would the detractors of the present struggle have been happy if there had been no reaction to the arrest of the leaders, if the country had calmly bowed its head before the imperialist jack-boot ? Or was it expected that only protest meetings should have been held demanding the release of arrested leaders (as was advocated by certain erstwhile Revolutionaries), and when they were not released further meetings should have been held, till the audience became too disgusted to attend, after which the "protestants" could have gone to sleep with a clear conscience ? If this be so, where was the sense of that brave resolution and those brave words that were poured forth from the lips of the greatest in the land at the Bombay A.I.C.C. ? If on the other hand this be not so, and if the people were expected to rise in answer to the British offensive, if, indeed, the arrest of the leaders was a signal for a mass struggle, then where is the grace and fairness in decrying the present struggle as un-Congress and unauthorised ? When you are on the war path, it is foolish to expect the enemy to allow you the leisure to complete all the formalities required by a peace-time constitution. It therefore appears to me to be mean and cowardly to attempt to show that the National struggle that started on the 9th of August, 1942, has not the authority and sanction of the Congress.

Jayaprakash Narayan's political involvements had never before been so hectic. Ever so often he went out on hurricane tours of the country, heavily disguised, constantly on the move so that no single indiscretion could catch up with him. It was also a time of great responsibility, and J.P. rose to the occasion with great strength of purpose. He wrote a spate of articles and pamphlets, carefully analysing the rapidly unfolding political situation, and addressing himself to every section of the people. His writings were simple, cogent and dazzlingly clear-cut, his own experience allowed him to identify with certain sections of people, and his relentless logic adopted their point of view.

In his underground, itinerant existence, Jayaprakash Narayan narrowly escaped being recognised and caught. In Benares, on one of his lightning tours, a strange thing happened. J.P. and Achyut Patwardhan had just moved out of a house where they had begun to feel at home. They moved next to the home of a *seth* where a political associate, Basavan Singh, disguised as another trader, had managed to find accommodation. Basavan Singh told his host that Jayaprakashji and Achyut Patwardhan were also traders, and asked if they could stay with him for a few days. The *seth* gave his consent. The next day, however, he came up to Basavan Singh and said, "But this is Jayaprakash Narayan ! How does he happen to be here ?" Basavan tried to convince the *seth* that he must be mistaken; but the man was adamant. He had heard him speaking in public many times, he could not possibly be wrong.

Basavan Singh said nothing. The *seth* then moved closer conspiringly and said that there was no cause for alarm. He was prepared to take the risk of keeping a wanted man in his house, but he told Basavan that the secret must be kept from his wife.

Later the same day, the *sethani* returned and met the guests. Drawing Basavan Singh aside, she said, "I know who that man is. He is Achyut Patwardhan. Don't worry though. I can keep a secret. But don't let the *seth* get to know". That night Jayaprakash Narayan and Achyut Patwardhan slipped away from the *seth's* house and found a place to stay elsewhere!

With the six escapees remaining at large, the Government announced that it had doubled the reward for their capture.

Jayaprakashji now had a price of Rs. 10,000 on his head. Yet his political work continued unabated.

At Delhi, Jayaprakashji attended an important meeting of the Central Co-ordinating Council of the movement. A host of intractable problems had to be attended to and sorted out. Commodities were disappearing from the markets, food was running short. Indian troops were getting demoralised—their spirits broken. In Calcutta, the Japanese bombardment had caused a severe dislocation of life. Transport and communications there were in a mess. It was essential to take stock of the situation, to recognise the situation for what it was, to build the revolution on the wreck of the past order. The meagre resources of militant nationalism had to be carefully harnessed and channelised so that it struck at the heart of the British dominion. Mistakes had to be rectified and lessons learnt. There was no underestimating the problems ahead.

At the Delhi meeting, the plan of raising a Freedom Brigade was mooted and approved. Sucheta Kripalani, on behalf of the Gandhians, expressed her dismay; but her dissent was brushed aside.

Further, the basis was laid for recruiting volunteers from among workers, peasants and students. Special attention had to be paid to the working class, because the communists were well entrenched in their ranks, and they made no secret of their misgivings of the movement. The peasantry all over the country cowered in fear—the double might of the *zamindars* and the British government had clubbed them into submission, and a special effort would have to be made to raise their spirits. Students had begun to trickle back into their colleges after the August movement had begun to appear hopeless and without direction. They too would have to be wooed back towards political activism. The army and police would have to be infiltrated and their sympathy gradually enlisted. Better methods of communication by radio and press would have to be devised and operated in secret. Jayaprakash Narayan assumed the task of raising a guerilla brigade, of educating it and preparing it for the struggle. Soon after these aims were agreed upon, he made preparations to leave for Nepal.

In the first flush of the August, 1942 uprising, small pockets of land had been liberated from the British, and Panchayati Raj had been proclaimed. For a very short period, these areas remained outside governmental control, but nothing was done to consolidate these victories. A few police *thanas* were looted, arms were seized, but as it became clear that the uprising in the rest of the country would not take place—Panchayati Raj came to an end.

It was clear to J.P. that spontaneous armed uprising was not enough. His task in Nepal was to raise and train a Freedom Brigade as a single-minded, disciplined force. Initially, it would be a small band of men, supplementing their resources through guerilla raids and surprise forays into India. Gradually, however, as they grew in experience and support, the force would grow until it came to represent the militant nationalism of the Indian people. The Resistance groups operating behind German lines in France and Poland furnished an operational blueprint of how the Freedom Brigade would work.

The guerilla squads were thus given a clear mission of destruction which would paralyse the machinery of the British Government. Three systems were singled out for destruction:

1) Disruption of communication lines including telegraph, telephone, mail and wireless lines, railways, roads, bridges and motor vehicles of the enemy;

2) Disruption of industrial plants, factories, mills and airports;

3) Incendiary activity, which covered destruction of government documents, buildings, petrol pumps, arms and ammunition by fire.

Guerilla units would suffice for most of these tasks, but industrial sabotage would require special people 'planted' among the permanent work force who could undertake their tasks without attracting attention.

The Freedom Brigade, as envisaged, was to be more effective than individual terrorist action. In the First Handbook, a special appeal was made to students and young revolutionaries to join the Brigade. Dr. Ram Manohar Lohia wrote in *Prepare for the Revolution.*

Units of five men, strong and educated, should be formed. As soon as the uprising takes place, these units will go

into the territories and lead the people and arrange for
concerted action. A disorganised populace that cannot
achieve its tasks even with the biggest sacrifices, will achieve
its aims under these task-forces. These units will be trained
to perform specialist tasks—seizure of arms and ammunition
from government depots, barricading a road, uprooting
railway lines, cutting telegraph wires, and leading assaults
on police *thanas*, jails, courts and secretariat buildings.
Wherever such forces are established, as soon as the revolution breaks out, the British Raj will collapse in a trice, and
other areas will quickly follow suit.

On the low-lying land near the river Kosi in Nepal, J.P.
lived in a thatched hut at a place called Bakro-Ka-Tapu. The
blueprint of the Brigade had been widely circulated, and
elicited a good response. Youths from Bihar, Bengal and the
eastern regions who had hitherto led an underground existence
as terrorists, began to arrive at this spot. More huts were
constructed for them to live in. The organisation started off
with two horses and a bullock-cart for its transport. Two dak
runners were engaged to carry messages into India. The camp
was situated at the base of a tall hill, which was selected as
the site of a radio transmitter, and the first broadcasts carrying
news of the revolution went on the air.

The first task force to be organised was the Bihar Freedom
Brigade. Suraj Narayan assumed the responsibility as co-
ordinator of the project. The whole province was scoured to
find volunteers, and immediately afterwards, training camps
were started. The first camp aimed at grooming an officer
cadre for the Brigade, men who would eventually be able to lead
independent columns of guerillas. Among this first group was
Nityanand, who was killed by a police bullet at Sonebarsa in
Bhagalpur (Bihar) some time later.

Jayaprakash had been at the camp for two months. The
training of a revolutionary cadre and the propoganda work by
radio were progressing smoothly. But about this time, the
British Government found out that Jayaprakash and Dr.
Lohia were in Nepal. It soon became known that the Government was pressurising the Nepalese Government to arrest all
the people involved in the venture. The camp began teeming
with British spies and intelligence agents. Any moment an

armed attack was expected.

J.P. and the others began to make frenzied preparations to abandon the site and move up into the mountains. J.P. was sent ahead to help raise some funds. The same day Shyam Nandan was arrested by a Nepalese armed unit. Jayaprakash, Dr. Lohia and two others were arrested a short while later, and they were taken across the Kosi towards Hanumannagar for interrogation.

This was in May 1944. In Hanumannagar, the prisoners were interrogated by a Nepalese magistrate. It was clear that his orders had come from the Government at Kathmandu, for repeatedly, he left the room to talk rapidly in Nepali on the telephone. The British intelligence had supplied him with photographs of the ring-leaders, and every now and again he peered anxiously into the prisoners' faces.

Jayaprakashji and the others stuck doggedly to their story that they were Bihari peasants fleeing from the injustice of British courts in India. Miraculously, the magistrate did not recognise the men from the photographs, and he was convinced that J.P. was not among them. Nevertheless, he would probably have handed them over to the British very soon, and they were kept behind bars for the night. News about the arrest reached the small force of armed men at the camp very quickly. They left for Hanumannagar the same day, 36 men in all, carrying with them their entire arsenal of three shotguns, one rifle, a stick of dynamite, two revolvers and pointed bamboo staves.

One whole day they spent planning their raid on the jail. At midnight, two men stole into the vicinity of the court-house and tried to find out where the men were kept captive. A sentry was overpowered, but his cry had alerted other guards, and very soon, the rescue force was fighting its way to the guard-room through a vicious cross-fire. It was a dark night, and the whole building had been plunged in utter darkness when the lights were hit by gunfire. Taken by surprise and thrown into utter confusion, the Nepalese sentries preferred to leave the area and alert the authorities. Meanwhile, the prisoners were set free from the guard room.

In rushing out, Lohia and Jayaprakash had run into a bramble bush and hurt their feet. Their escape was thus slow, but by evening of the next day, they had re-crossed the Kosi and took shelter in an *Ahir's* house in the evening.

The next day they moved on again, skirting police outposts, sticking to the woods. Then at Radhopur, they hired a bullock-cart and headed in the direction of Bengal. The following day, the men broke up, and boarded separate trains for Calcutta.

The countrywide search by the Government for J.P. was not relaxed. Whenever, wherever, it was suspected that he might be hiding, the police raided shops, houses, hotels. Gradually, legends of mythical powers began to surround his name. Rumours spread that he was a man who could change his shape at will, that he moved about surrounded by an army of bodyguards, that he kept the British troops at bay by chanting *mantras . . . .*

Sir Reginald Maxwell, the Home Secretary in the British India Government at that time, was bent on recapturing Jayaprakash Narayan, dead or alive—preferably dead.

Before he went on his famous 21-day fast, in a letter to the British Government, Gandhi wrote :

. . . The Congressmen who have been fighting for India's liberty for over half a century would have flocked to the allied banner as one man for the defence of India's freedom newly won. But the Government did not wish to treat India as an equal partner and an ally. They put out of action those who made this demand. Some of them are even being hounded, as if they were dangerous criminals. I have in mind Sri Jayaprakash Narayan and others like him. A reward of Rs. 5,000, now doubled, had been promised to the informant who would show his hiding place. I have taken Sri Jayaprakash Narayan purposely as my illustration because, as hearsay rightly says, he differs from me on several fundamentals. But my differences, great as they are, do not blind me to his indomitable courage and his sacrifice of all that a man held dear for the love of his country. I have read his manifesto which is given as an appendix to the indictment. Though I cannot subscribe to some of the views therein, it breathes nothing but burning patriotism and his impatience of foreign domination. It is a virtue of which any country would be proud.

By the end of 1943, a pall of gloom had begun to settle on the nationalist agitation. The Freedom Brigade had been disbanded. Fifty thousand people languished in jails in different parts of the country. Every week the roster of fresh arrests grew larger. Slowly, the police cordon was tightening around the few leaders who remained at large.

Jayaprakash Narayan was advised by his associates to leave the country for a while, or else to lie low somewhere until the police had given up the search, or at least until a fresh agitation preoccupied the attentions of the Government. But although his health was poor and the damp weather had started, Jayaprakash Narayan's relentless travelling continued without let up.

The Punjab had not been a major participant in the 1942 movement. J.P. decided that this was one area that needed a transfusion of nationalist feeling, and he went to Delhi en route to Lahore in September 1944.

Somehow, the Delhi Police learnt of J.P.'s intentions and searched a number of apartments in Delhi, but Jayaprakash had already left Delhi by the Frontier Mail. All night, as the train rushed westwards, Jayaprakash was not disturbed. Early in the morning, at Amritsar station, he ordered some tea and bought a newspaper. An Englishman and two Sikhs got into his compartment, and he did not pay them much attention.

When the train left the station, the Englishman began talking to J.P. For a while, they played cat and mouse. . .but then the Englishman said, "You are Jayaprakash Narayan. You are under arrest." Jayaprakash Narayan wore a surprised, offended look, and continued to protest that he was a merchant from Bombay on his way to Rawalpindi. His baggage, bedding, pillows and clothes were searched, and William Robinson, the S.P. of Lahore was surprised that J.P. was not armed. He warned him : "If you resist in any way, I have orders to shoot you." Jayaprakash shrugged his shoulders and continued to look surprised and innocent.

When the train stopped at Mughalpura station, Jayaprakash's hands were strapped to his holdall, and he was escorted off the train into a waiting police car that took him to Lahore Fort.

On the 14th of December, 1943, Jayaprakash was declared a State prisoner, and his interrogation began. The Government did not want it to be known that Jayaprakash Narayan was imprisoned at Lahore Fort. But as the news of his capture and subsequent torture spread, his friends went into action. From Bombay, the well-known barrister Pardivala came to the Punjab and filed a writ of *habeas-corpus* in the Lahore High Court. Soon after, the Punjab police arrested Pardivala and quashed the writ. Next Purnima Banerjee came to Lahore and hired a locally famous lawyer, Jeevanlal Kapur, to file another writ. The Government bent backwards to avoid the consequence of this action. First J.P.'s standing as a 'security prisoner' was altered to that of 'State Prisoner by Regulation 3 of 1918', whereby *habeas-corpus* did not apply. And then as soon as the writ was withdrawn, Jayaprakash became 'security prisoner again.'

While he was in Lahore Fort. J.P. kept a diary, which was later published by the Socialist Book Centre in Madras. The first page in the diary is dated 17th February 1944, and began with the signature of a prison official and the cryptic legend: 'The notebook has been paged and it contains 52 pages'. The diary is an account of his life in jail, faithfully recorded at the end of each day.

Jayaprakash was allowed to receive two newspapers: the *Tribune* and the *Statesman*. The newsheets, however, looked more like ribbons than pages, because news about the progress of the war, Indian legislative reporting and the editorials were carefully cut out before he received the papers. Much of his diary echoes his frustration of not knowing what was happening in the world outside and his speculations about what was taking place.

The diary also contains the first draft of Jayaprakash's letter to the Home Secretary, Government of Punjab, in February 1944:

Sir,
 ...I was arrested on the 18th of September last year at Amritsar and brought the same day to this Fort. After a month of my detention here I was taken to the office where the officers

of the Punjab, Bihar and Bengal C.I.D.s were present . . . . In this manner, my so-called interrogation began. Thereafter, I was taken to the office every day and made to sit there for varying periods of time. . . .I pointed out to the interrogators that forcing me to sit in the office for hours together and repeatedly asking me questions that I had declined to answer was a form of harassment to which they had no right to subject me. I was told I was in the hands of the Punjab C.I.D. and the question of rights did scarcely arise. Gradually the hours of interrogation—in plain language, harassment—were lengthened : from 8 a.m. to midnight. . . . The final stage in my harassment, which turned into a form of torture, was to allow me no sleep during day or night . . . . I can assure you in all honesty that, when continued for days, it is a most oppressive and nerve-racking experience. I cannot describe it as anything but torture . . . .

My grievance is that I have been tortured and treated in this fashion without any justification or warrant whatever. There is and there can be no moral or legal sanction for it....

Suppression of political opponents is the essence of Nazism and Fascism—torture of political prisoners is their most characteristic feature. I am conscious of the argument that those who believe in violence as a political method, as I do, must be prepared to be forcibly suppressed. I grant that, but there are lawful means even for such suppression. A political revolutionary may be executed for his offences when found guilty by the established law, but he may not be put to any torture for the extraction of information....A prisoner of war has certain rights and immunities which civilised society scrupulously respects. The same person who would be most mercilessly bayonetted to death on the battle-field would be immune from illtreatment in the war prisoners' camp and would receive such amenities as the standards of the countries concerned and his own status would warrant. . . .

I remain,
Yours faithfully,
Jayaprakash Narayan

8th May, 1944 : 'I am not rejoicing because I expect Gandhiji's release (from prison) will lead to some kind of understanding with the British. In this time of struggle and war, I do not

want any understanding to take place. Because in these conditions any pact cannot be good for Indian Independence. I
hope Gandhi will not enter into any pact that will not be
good for our goal of complete Independence.'

The question posed by Gandhi's release evidently troubled
J.P. a great deal, because around this date his diary is filled
with his ruminations about the possible implications of
Gandhi's presence to the developments in the Muslim League,
Congress and the British.

Gandhi and the Congress had publicly disowned the August
(1942) movement, perhaps because it had not been successful.
This thought troubled J.P. a great deal, and occupied many
pages of his diary.

For 16 months, Jayaprakash Narayan remained in Lahore
Fort. Not only was he cut off from the world outside, he did
not have access to the other prisoners in the Fort. It took him
some time to realise that Dr. Lohia too was detained in the
same compound. And then, in 1945, Jayaprakash and Lohia
were removed to Agra Jail on an indefinite sentence.

The chief of a British Parliamentary delegation who met
Jayaprakash and Lohia in the Agra Jail humorously described the encounter:

We entered the Jail in the evening, passing through
huge spiked, iron gates, padlocked for security. We were
led to a small courtyard, surrounded on all four sides by
massive, unscalable walls. It was here that Dr. Lohia and
Jayaprakash were brought by an escort of armed guards.
Chairs were brought for us to sit on, and they were arranged in a circle, with the prisoners in the centre. We talked
to them for about two hours. The Jail Superintendent and
other officials stood at a respectful distance, not wanting
to hamper the talks, but ready to deal with an emergency.
Before it was dark, two big hurricane lanterns were brought
to the courtyard, though they only succeeded in creating
a dull, smoky light. It was a strange scene—the tiny courtyard, and the towering walls. In the semi-darkness, a
group of warders, and in front of them, the member of the
British Parliamentary delegation talking to a pair of dangerous Indian prisoners undergoing indefinite sentence. After

the talks, the warders breathed a sigh of relief that nothing had gone amiss.

We then peeped into the dingy cells in which the prisoners were housed. There was very little furniture or personal belongings, but there was a treasure-house of books on poetry, philosophy, art and sociology . . . . If these two had compromised even a little with their proclaimed belief and programme, they would have been released long ago. But they will never do that, because they maintain that there are some things more important than personal freedom, and they will not budge an inch.

They shook hands with us happily and bade good-bye. It was though we had been to see them as visitors on our excursion, and now they were returning to their solitary confinement.

Soon after remours began to spread that J.P. would be pardoned and released, though this was clearly not possible until the British Cabinet Mission came to India. It was also said that Gandhi had demanded Jayaprakash's release on proof of the sincerity of the British Government.

In April, the Home Member of the Indian Government met Jayaprakash in the Agra Jail. After a long discussion, Jayaprakash was asked whether he would resort to violence to win Independence. He answered: "We want independence—if we can achieve that through *ahimsa*, then that will be good. But if necessary we will not shrink from using violence to attain our ends."

On the 11th April, 1946, the whole country was electrified at the news that Jayaprakash Narayan and Dr. Lohia had been released from the Agra Jail. The two men were given a tumultuous welcome.

From Agra J.P. went to Delhi, where he met and conferred with members of the British Cabinet Mission. From Delhi, he was due to go to Patna, but the huge welcome which residents of that city had planned for J.P. was not yet ready, and it was contrived to delay J.P. at Benares to allow a few more days for the preparations.

When J.P. finally arrived at Patna, he was overwhelmed by the massive crowds, the festooned streets and cries of *Jayaprakash Zindabad* ! *Inquilab Zindabad* ! *August Kranti Zinda-*

bad ! Ramdhari Singh Dinkar read out a poem to the assembled people, and J.P. was pressed to make a speech. He
said :

> I know this much, that all of you are paying homage
> not to me, but to the spirit of the August revolution. When
> I was in jail, I used to wonder about where the support
> for further work would come from. But your enthusiasm
> has convinced me that you are all ready to participate in
> this struggle, that you share my faith and purpose . . . .
> If the present negotiations with the British fail, then the
> Congress must begin another struggle against the British
> rule, in the same manner as 1931. The Government knows
> this and is preparing for it. A list of names has been drawn
> up. The police *thanas* have begun stockpiling arms and
> weapons. Why are we then waiting idly for the Govern-
> ment to strike first ? We must be fully prepared to
> resist . . . . During the August revolt, the Indian sepoys
> at Jamshedpur went on strike in sympathy with our cause,
> and the Government had to call in English reserves. The
> Congress leaders point to the failure of the August move-
> ment, but they do not realise the extent of our success.
> Very few countries have experienced a movement like ours.
> Nearly 40,000 men laid down their lives in this revolution,
> and we are chastised for not adopting non-violence. The
> Congress is proving to be wary of seizing its chances . . . .
> It has pained me that ever since the Congress has been out-
> lawed, its programme has fallen to pieces, it has given up
> its revolutionary objectives and now is preoccupied with the
> elections and negotiations of compromise . . . .

Meanwhile, the Cabinet Mission concluded its talks with
Maulana Azad, Jinnah, Gandhi and the representatives of all
the parties and communities. Jinnah started the negotiations
with his emphatic demand for a Pakistan consisting of the six
'Muslim' Provinces. The alternative which the Mission put
before Jinnah were either to accept a small Pakistan with full
sovereign status or a large Pakistan *within* an Indian union and
with less sovereign powers.

As the position of the League and the Congress began to
harden (Jinnah was clamouring against the conception of a
"moth-eaten" Pakistan) the Cabinet Mission began to work

out a constitution which struck a balance between a strong, united India and an independent Pakistan—if that was possible ! The Ministers were faced with the Congress-League disagreement on almost every point of detail.

On the 16th May, 1946 the mission published its plan rejecting the division of the country into two separate and sovereign states, yet taking into account the fears of the communal minority by devising three separate bodies to draw up a constitution. Britain was to transfer power to India soon after the Indian constituent assembly had framed a constitution. Meanwhile, the administration was to be carried on by an Interim Government consisting of the representatives of the Indian political parties.

There could be no agreement on the composition of the Interim Government, though the Congress Working Committee accepted the Mission's long-term plan on the 25th June, 1946. On the 7th July that year the All-India Congress Committee met in Bombay to endorse the Working Committee's resolution of the 25th June (1946). It was at this meeting that Nehru took over the Congress Presidency from Maulana Azad. On the same day the Congress Socialists attacked the Cabinet Mission plan, calling it a trap laid by the British imperialists, and asked the Congress Committee to reject it. Nehru with the intention of defending Congress' acceptance of the plan, chose to make an equally fiery and provocative speech which led to immediate misconstructions. Jinnah saw Nehru's statements as a complete repudiation of the Cabinet Mission plan, and condemned the Congress for its "pettifogging and haggling attitude." Immediately, he called for 16th August (1946) as 'direct action' day and a wave of communal rioting began. Five thousand people were killed in Calcutta in 48 hours of rioting—it was the beginning of a tidal wave of killing that reached gigantic proportions of half a million before it was spent.

J.P. and the Congress Socialists were aghast at the developments. Now that there was a real chance of establishing a government that was not merely a figure-head, the Congress and the League were frittering away their energies in bitter conflict. J.P. made it clear that he had no truck with either of the two bodies: he castigated the Congress sharply for sacrificing its revolutionary goals, and the League for stabbing the objective of complete independence in the back.

Soon, however, it became apparent that the 'working arrangement' between the Congress and the C.S.P. had outlived its utility. The C.S.P. had served as a useful counterfoil to the Forward Bloc and the communists. The relationship had now worn threadbare, and this was becoming painfully obvious to the Socialists.

In February 1947, the Congress Socialist Party had a session at Kanpur to weigh the consequences of the 'shift in Congress' attitude'. Smarting under the implications of a recent Congress resolution that 'now the members of *other* parties can no longer be counted as Congressites,' the C.S.P. responded by dropping the name 'Congress': now it was merely the 'Socialist Party'! Dr. Lohia, as President of the session, addressed the delegates :

> The deletion of the word *Congress* does not mean opposition to the Congress. The Congress has represented our nationalist organisation. The condition of Congress membership, as a pre-requisite of joining our Party, has been removed. This does not mean that we have left the Congress. But by dropping the word *Congress*, people who agree with our programme but do not want to join the Congress, are enabled to join us formally . . . our ties with the Congress have not snapped, they have merely become slack.

> The Congress is our home. Even when one leaves a home, it is not easy to speak badly of it. We cannot break down a house in which we have lived for so many years. We have contributed to the splendour of the Congress, we cannot now turn around and blacken its face . . . . The Congress hankers after Ministerial office . . . . I do not accept a total severance of ties with the Congress. It is our hope that as long as Gandhi lives, he will not allow the Congress to abandon its revolutionary goals . . . .

On February 20, 1947 the British Labour Government announced its plan that power would be transferred to Indians by a date not later than June 1948. Lord Wavell, the viceroy, returned to England and the last of the British Governor-Generals in India, Lord Mountbatten, arrived in India with a definite mission : to wind up the 182-year-old British Indian empire in 15 months.

Mountbatten spent his first weeks in the country meeting the Indian leaders individually. The first interview with Nehru was rewarding, and mutual confidence and friendship were established between them. On the thorny question of a United India versus Pakistan the decision was made for the latter. The Congress High Command—specifically, Nehru and Patel—had reconciled themselves to Partition in some form by the end of 1946. Now that they were at the threshold of power they felt inclined to accept Pakistan rather than go back and continue the struggle for India's unity. To the end, Gandhi fought a rearguard battle to save India from Partition, but the Congress did not accept his plan.

At one point, knowing J.P.'s identical feelings about Partition, Gandhi asked Nehru to elect J.P. as Congress President in June 1947. Nehru did not agree, and Rajendra Prasad became the President of the Party instead.

The Congress opposed this resolution, and it was dropped without a vote. Gandhi bowed to the feeling against him, and urged unity. What was the C.S.P. to do ? Once again, as at Tripura, it declined to vote on the issue. In later years, this was a course which the socialists were to bitterly regret.

In August 1946, Jayaprakash Narayan recorded his alarm at the rapid pace of events which threatened to engulf all that the Congress had stood for. His views were set out in a third letter to the Fighters for Freedom :

Aware of what President Nehru has described as the compulsion of facts, i.e., aware of the limitations of its sovereignty, aware of its weaknesses, aware of the British stooges and enemies of freedom and democracy in its ranks, aware of the presence of the British Army and British Viceroy—aware of all this and more, the Constituent Assembly might choose to tread what I am sure is going to be described as the path of realism. In other words, the Assembly might decide to make compromise after compromise producing in the end neither freedom, nor democracy, nor national unity. So, the nation, thwarted and disillusioned, would have to turn once again to the path from which it is being misled today—the path of revolutionary action, the path of resistance and struggle, the straight but difficult path of freedom.

Thus we see in either case. i.e., whether the Constituent Assembly "succeeds" or whether it fights and "fails", or a struggle for freedom is inevitable. Anyone who has a correct appreciation of the present co-relation of forces in this country should not find it difficult to accept this conclusion. Today, it is still possible for British imperialism to face us with the "compulsion of facts". Till this "compulsion" is removed by revolutionary action, freedom would be an illusion. Nor can anyone expect to change the facts of the present situation by argument, concession and diplomatic finesse.

We, therefore, reach the conclusion—and it will bear repetition—that the struggle for freedom does not cease with the acceptance of the British constitutional proposals. That struggle will continue. In fact, the character and scope of that struggle will become deeper and wider. To the struggle for liberty will be added the struggle for national unity and bread.

Acceptance of the British proposals will let loose many forces of national disintegration. It is commonly supposed that one positive contribution that the British have made to Indian polity is to unify the country; and it is a common lament that they foolishly enough are bent today upon destroying that monument of their noble work. Nothing could be greater folly than this view. Far from creating unity in Indian life the British have always done their best to divide us; to divide Hindus and Muslims, to divide Harijans from other Hindus, to create a Sikh minority, to detach princely India from the rest of the country, to set the princes agaist the people, to bolster up the Zamindars into pillars of British rule, to bribe Capital and the middle class to turn into enemies of their country....

...Secondly, the impending constitutional changes are bound to bring two the fore, economic and class issues. The form of Swaraj, the question, 'Swaraj for whom' will no longer remain academic or remote questions, but will become matters of immediate and urgent importance demanding immediate answers and affecting all our politics not theoretically but practically. That is, the struggle for bread, always an integral part of the struggle for freedom, will move up to the front line and acquire

an importance no less than any other.

...As matters stand, the common struggle of the people would have to be waged in the context of a Constituent Assembly, possibly an Interim Government, and later on in the context of a Union Government, Group and Provincial governments.

The Congress, of which we are a part, seems likely to be associated with all these developments. As such, it seems certain that the Congress struggle for liberty, unity and bread will be conducted, if at all, through the constitutional and state machinery. Already the Congress is being converted into a parliamentary party. If this process goes on to its logical conclusion, there can be little doubt that the Congress must fail to achieve much success in this three-fold struggle. A constitutional and administrative machinery might be of use in certain circumstances, but situated as we are, the people's struggle must be carried on mainly outside the legislatures and the portals of government departments.

To carry on this struggle is our job today—the job of all the fighters for freedom.

Jayaprakash Narayan's fear was twofold—firstly, that the British might contrive to stay on in India despite their assurances ; or if they did go, they would leave behind a truncated State, having let loose all the divisive tendencies that paraded before the British as independent spokesmen for castes, princes, communities and religions. If the latter became a reality, Jayaprakash knew that the Congress would fall a prey to becoming a party to the division. It was a gloomy insight, but one which anticipated the logic of communal representation and political haggling. Jayaprakash anticipated the fact that Nehru and Patel had grown old and tired in the struggle, and now that they were at the threshold of power, they would be inclined to accept Pakistan rather than go back and continue their work for India's unity.

The Indian Constituent Assembly was convened late on the night of the 14th August, 1947 to assume sovereignty at midnight, the exact moment of India's independence. The midnight hour struck and celebrations started all over India. The British Raj had reached its last moment. It was a glorious event, one for which men like Jayaprakash Narayan had fought—but it also meant tragedy and bloodshed on an un-paralleled scale: Bengal, Bihar and Punjab were aflame, millions lost their homes and their families. And as a bitter climax to these terrible events, Gandhi, the crusader for peace, was shot dead on the 30th January, 1948.

Just one day before Gandhiji's assassination, Prabhavati had left his side to join Jayaprakashji in Patna. Two days later, she was back in Delhi, sobbing her heart out as Bapu's cortege winded its way to the funeral ground. J.P. stood next to her, his eyes clouded with grief and sorrow.

Chapter Five

THE constitutional foundations of a new India were being laid. For weeks, the Constituent Assembly put together the fabric of a document which would shape the destiny of a new nation. Jayaprakash, however, did not accept the membership of the Assembly. He felt that its members did not represent the people.

Soon after Gandhi's death, in March 1948, the Congress announced that no member of another party could remain within the Congress. To the Socialists, this meant marching orders.

In the same month, the Socialists held a Party caucus at Nasik, at which they hit back at the Congress. The crucial resolution read:

The Congress is incapable of further changing its class character and becoming an instrument of socialism because of its total identification with Government and its refusal to support the social struggles of the masses . . . . The Congress is in danger, because of its authoritarian bias, of being overwhelmed by anti-secular, anti-democratic forces of the Right. Hence, for the maintenance of a democratic climate, an opposition becomes necessary. The Socialist Party alone can provide this opposition which continues the tradition of identification with the struggles of the dispossessed.

Jayaprakash recorded his own views, which had already moved closer to Gandhism:

128

   The theory that all politics are power politics has the
necessary underlying base . . . that the state is the only
instrument of social good. In other words, those who subscribe to this theory believe that they must capture the
State in order to be able to serve society and bring about
the social transformation they desire . . . . I reject this view
completely . . . . The experience of totalitarian countries
has shown that if the State is looked upon as the sole agent
of social transformation, we get nothing but a regimented
society in which the State is all powerful and popular
initiative is extinct and the individual is made a cog in a
vast inhuman machine . . . . Democracy requires that the
people should depend as little as possible on the State. And,
both according to Mahatma Gandhi and Karl Marx, the
highest stage of democracy is that in which the State has
withered away . . . .

Clearly, J.P. has come a long way from the time when
he had said in *Why Socialism* that 'No party in the world of
today can build up socialism unless it has the machinery of
the State in its hands.' The change in J.P.'s views was not lost
on the delegates at Nasik, and they criticised his report from
an orthodox Marxist standpoint. J.P. was unrepentent. He
had begun to ask fundamental questions about materialist
exegesis—the road towards Gandhism was opening out.

   In 1946, the Socialists had been elected to the Legislative Assembly in U. P. as Congressites. Now that a parting of
the ways had come, the Socialists resigned their seats and prepared to fight the by-elections. The Congress put up its own
candidates to oppose its erstwhile allies; in its electoral campaign, the Congress fought shy of taking a stand on current
political issues—instead, it attacked the Socialists on grounds
which bore no relevance to concrete issues. Narendra Dev, for
instance, was debunked for being an atheist, an opponent of
dharma and culture. His Congress rival was projected as the
apotheosis of Indian culture and values. There could be no
greater mockery of an electoral platform.

   J.P. threw himself into the campaign with great vigour.
From the *zila* (district) upwards, a new Party had to be organised and projected as a separate entity whereas the Congress,
because of its identification with the freedom struggle, stood to

reap the laurels of an established and victor party. New Socialist cadres had to be trained, new workers inducted into the
Party, a whole new campaign to be devised and launched. At
the end of the by-elections, despite winning about 42% of
the total votes polled, the Socialists won none of the seats in
the United Provinces.

After this defeat, the Socialists withdrew to lick their
wounds. "I had often wondered," said J.P. at the time, "if I
would have voted Socialist if I had been an ordinary peasant.
I think I would not have. Why? Because I would know nothing
at all about this Party. Before the elections, no Socialist had
come to my village, they had done nothing at all for me, I had
no reason to be grateful to them."

But how then had the Socialists managed to win such
a large percentage of the total votes ? Clearly, the reason
was that a number of Socialist candidates were individually
well known, and commanded great respect. But as a party, the
Socialists had had no time to separate their identity from that
of the Congress. In the cities and large towns the Socialists
had done creditably well—but they lost heavily in the countryside, in the small villages that made up the bulk of the
electorate.

Only in a few particular spheres were the Socialists well-
known. Because of their work in the Kisan Sabha movement,
they were strong in Bihar and U.P.; in a few universities
in Bombay and northern India they had a sizeable following.
And the Trade Union movement had established them among
the industrial unions. But that was all; compared to the
national following of the Congress in the first flush of Independence, their pockets of influence counted as nothing.

Having been so rudely reminded of their organisational
shortcomings, the Socialist Party got down to the task of rebuilding the party organs. Dr. Lohia and J.P. began a
round of whirlwind tours. They found that there tours were
much more difficult than those they had undertaken during
the nationalist movement. While the British were in India,
they had preached a war of Independence—the message was
clear and unambiguous. But now that the Raj had come to
an end, it was difficult for the average voter to sort out the
myriad strands of political principles which divided the candi-

dates one from another.

Prabhaji, who now travelled wherever J.P. went, recorded in her diary; 'Because of his role in the August Revolt, he is welcomed enthusiastically wherever he goes. Whether it is Central India, Madras or Maharashtra, he gets very big audiences. . . .so far we have travelled 550 miles by car, sixty hours by train, participated in 30 *sabhas* (meetings), forty speeches, and we have collected from the people Rs. 2,00,811. . .'

From early 1948 until 1950-51, J.P. and Dr. Lohia were immersed in the task of rebuilding the Socialist Party. Their line was that the country had won a sham victory. 'Before Independence', J.P. told the crowds, 'I had said that we will not win *swaraj* through an "understanding" with the British. I was wrong—we have got *swaraj*. But is this true independence ? I had never visualised that Lahore would not be part of a free India. Nor that the banks of the Ravi, where we first vowed to fight for full independence, would not be in India. Nor that Gandhi would not be here. . . .'

As the breach between the Congress and the Socialists widened, the latter grew openly critical of the new Government's temerity in implementing the ideals which had been enunciated before 1947. Between 1948 and 1952, J.P. and Nehru continued to correspond, but there was a sharp edge to their differences, and a glint of steel in the recriminations they exchanged.

In 1949, the pace of events quickened for the Socialists. A major session of the Party was organised at Patna. The programme of the Party was subjected to scrutiny and was overhauled. J.P. wrote a report on the constitution suggesting far-reaching changes in criteria of membership of the Party. In order to carve out an independent domain for themselves, J.P. suggested that they had to draw their nourishment from the organisation of industrial workers, peasants and craftsmen. Elitism, as a method of running the Party, had to be shaken off. And finally, a draft resolution containing the objectives of the Party was prepared and circulated—'Forward' was the watchword.

Within the Party, a small but vocal section was critical of the decision to participate in the democratic institutions of the State. It put forward the view that India was not a true democracy, and that the Socialists would be effectively curbed and repressed unless it chose to opt out of the parliamentary system. Violent revolution was the only answer. J.P., and the majority, aligned themselves against this view, and secured a vote in favour of broadening the base of Party membership. The Socialist Party, they maintained, had to put themselves forward as a democratic alternative to the Congress. Contesting the elections would serve as a process of political tutelage for the masses. Therefore, the Party had to strengthen itself in order to win at the polls.

In New Delhi, the finishing touches to the Indian Constitution were being debated and incorporated. But on the food front, the Government faced its first real crisis. In the coffee-houses of the capital, there was talk of a joint government being formed to meet the grave situation. The rumour was that members of the Opposition would be invited to share the responsibility of Government.

In September 1949, J.P. was touring Bombay and Maharashtra. Speculation about a Joint Ministry had reached fever-pitch when J.P. was in Bombay city, and he was asked to make a statement to the *Blitz* and the U.P.I. He said :

The Socialist Party would be prepared to work and cooperate with any other political party towards solving the country's problems. However, in the present situation of the Congress rule, and the way in which 15 Ministries have been constituted in the States, a Joint Ministry is not possible. The Congress Party has not indicated any interest in a Joint Ministry, and the whole question is academic. Today the situation is that the Congress has a big majority in the State Assemblies, and the Socialist representation is almost nothing. Under these circumstances, talk of a Joint Ministry does not make sense.

Later the same month, J.P. went to Bangalore to attend the National Working Committee session of the Socialist Party. Immediately afterwards, the General Council of the Party met in session, with Yusuf Meherally as President. Important resolutions on the new revolutionary Government in China were passed. J.P. expressed his disappointment at the progress of Party organisation since the meeting at Patna. He also sternly rebuked those 'counsellors of doom' in the party who, extrapolating from their failure at the polls, denounced the parliamentary, democratic way. True, the Socialists had suffered another defeat in the District Board elections in Madras Province. But they had also some success to boast of, in the Bombay Corporation elections, and J.P. reaffirmed the intention of the Party to continue to appeal to the people at the hustings.

At this meeting, the delegates also formulated their attitude towards Congress' achievements since coming to power. The Congress, they said, had gone over to the counter-revolutionary camp and allied itself with the big bourgeoisie. J.P. compared the achievements of Attlee's Labour Government to that of the Congress, and concluded that the latter was not going to stick to its promises of nationalising major industries and public utility services in the country. He added : 'The people of this country will not be free until there is an absolute change in the character of the Central Government. The need of the hour is for a purposeful, strong Party in opposition, and we will fulfil this need.'

In November 1949, the Socialists staged an impressive show of strength in Patna. Nearly 50,000 peasants from all over Bihar converged on the city on the 23rd of that month. Many of them carried red flags. On the night of the 24th November, they set out in a torchlight procession from the Socialist Party offices and marched through the city. The next day, the peasants gathered in Gandhi *maidan* to listen to speeches by the Socialist leaders. Ramanand Mishra addressed the rally : 'You have come here from every corner of Bihar. Many of you have come on foot. There are many examples of similar marches in history. In situations of hardship, when great numbers of men have wanted to bring about change, they have marched like you have. And they have shaken the world. Your efforts too, will not be without significance. . . .'

J.P. too addressed the mammoth crowd :

'Friends, I want to begin by warning you of certain dangers. You have raised a few slogans that sadden me. You said *Long live Jayaprakash.* I do not like you to cheer in this way. During the Independence movement, you cheered Nehru and Patel in similar fashion. What happened after that ? You were disappointed, you felt deceived. For this reason, I say : do not cheer individuals, do not think that individual statesmen will save you. You have to find the strength within yourself to change society. You are the agents of history.

That so many of you have gathered here today is proof that the people have courage, that they will march forward. Your slogans are against the present regime. Today, Patel and Nehru shape the destinies of our country. Why is there so much unrest ? Because their Government is the Government of the rich. I am not talking about corruption. Even if all the people were honest, the Government would still not be your Government. It is a Government for the rich. . .'

The peasant rally was a success, but the Party could not relax its organisational efforts. The only way to combat the Congress was to develop strong roots among the organised sector of labour, and among the small peasantry—this had become an article of faith in the socialist creed.

In June 1950, the annual session of the Socialist Party was held in Madras. Asoka Mehta was President, in the absence of Meherally. Narendra Dev was ill, and could not attend. Dr. Lohia sent in his report from Bombay, but did not personally attend.

In many ways, it was a key moment in the history of the Party. It was at this session that the differences between J.P. and Dr. Lohia came out in the open.

The immediate cause of disagreement was the Korean War which had broken out in June 1950. The foreign affairs committee of the Party met in Bombay to decide its attitude towards developments in the Far East, and Dr. Lohia put forward the view that the Party should not take sides with America, or its communist enemies in Soviet Russia and China. J.P. was vehemently against 'sitting on the fence'. This disagreement flared up into a major rift, and Dr. Lohia stayed away from the Madras Conference.

In Madras, the Korean question was the subject of intense debate. Ultimately, a majority voted with J.P. in support of Nehru's official statements condemning American aggression in Korea. Thereafter, Dr. Lohia published his dissenting views in the newspapers.

At the Madras session, J.P. read a paper on 'Democratic Socialism' which represented an advance on his paper at Nasik. Affirming the Party's commitment to 'democratic' as opposed to 'totalitarian' socialism, he added :

. . . the Policy statement has distinguished the democratic method from constitutionalism. The Socialist Party is not a mere parliamentary party. As a matter of fact, the Socialist Party hardly exists in the Parliament. The Party is a revolutionary party and while it may use the parliamentary method it depends for its success on its work outside Parliament and among the people.

While it is a part of the democratic method to capture Parliament through elections and to form a government, the Socialist Party believes that a social revolution, even after the capture of power, would have to be carried out by the people themselves, aided and guided as they may be by the Socialist State.... It will not make the least difference to me if the Party were completely swept off the board (in the elections).

In 1951-52, the country was busy preparing for the first General Elections. All organisational, propagandist, supportive political activity was timed to reach a frenzied climax just before the polling. In the conclaves of the Socialist Party, J.P. noticed an attitude which he condemned—many party workers, impatient for quick results, felt that their elections would either make or break the Party. The future of the Party, they said, was premised on its performance in these elections. To J.P., this was an irrational thought—it was more important that the party should keep to its ideals than that its supporters should demand immediate gains. There was no under-estimating the travails of building up a strong, committed party organisation.

In the midst of his hectic activities, J.P.'s health collapsed, and he went to Madras to recuperate. He returned to elec-tioneering a month later.

Late in 1951, J.P. made an attempt to create a joint platform of all the democratic and socialist parties in opposition to the Congress. He did not succeed; nevertheless, the Socialists were confident of having made major gains, particularly in Bihar.

On the 4th of January, 1952 the country went to the polls. Seventy-seven political parties contested the elections, in many cases blurring the choice placed before the voter. The results were a great disappointment to the Opposition parties—the Congress won 362 out of 489 seats to the Lok Sabha, though it won only 45 per cent of the votes cast. This distortion came from the single non-transferable vote system which was adopted as the electoral procedure. The Socialists won 15 per cent of the votes both in the Parliament and State elections, but they had spread themselves thinly, and won very few seats. With only half as many votes, the Communists, by concentrating their effort, won twice as many Parliamentary seats as the Socialists.

The Socialists were utterly dismayed at the results. Soon after the elections, the Party summoned delegates for a meeting in Patna. Before the proceedings began, Ram Nandan Mishra circulated a pamphlet which analysed the causes of their defeat in Marxian terms. He argued that, primarily because of J.P., the Party had eschewed the class-struggle as a means of mobilising sentiment and support in the elections. 'J.P.', he said, 'is a friend of Jawaharlal's. He has helped the Congress to win these elections.' J.P. had become the scapegoat for the Party's failure.

In May, 1952, at another Party session in Panchmarhi, Dr. Lohia addressed the delegates on the subject of voluntary land donations. This was an attempt to forge some kind of a bridge between the activity of the Party in the rural areas, and that of the Sarvodaya workers.

At the same meeting, J.P. announced that he would gift half of the 50 acres he owned in Sitab Diyara to landless peasants.

Expressing his agreement with Dr. Lohia, he said at that meeting : 'This line of thought will help us overcome some of the shortcomings in our socialist programme . . . . The Sarvodaya workers are at this point in the same condition as the Congress Party. They are driven by various conflicting points of view. Some of them are attracted towards communism, some identify with the Congress, and one group is closer to us in its thinking. This group within the Sarvodaya organisation wants to cooperate with the Socialists.'

In June 1952, J.P. was instrumental in arranging a parliamentary alliance between the Kisan Mazdoor Praja Party and the Socialist Party. In September that year, the General Council of the Socialist Party, meeting in Bombay, voted to merge the two organisations in view of their common ideals, and the Praja Samajwadi Party (PSP) was born. Acharya Kripalani became its first President.

Vinoba Bhave, Gandhi's spiritual heir, began the *bhoodan*, or land-gift movement in 1951. In its conception, it was both a concrete answer to the problem of the landless, and a movement of 'spiritual regeneration.' Independent of Government action, it set out to collect land by persuasion, to change the hearts of the rich, to develop village self-rule and autonomy. Jayaprakash Narayan paid a visit to Vinobaji in district Banda (U.P.) in June that year and came away deeply impressed. He left only because he had decided to go on a three week fast to purify himself. With him, in Poona, were Prabhavati and J.P.'s secretary and friend, Mahavir Prasad Sinha. The fast was begun on the 22nd June that year at 9.30 in the morning. Mahavir Prasad in the letters to his wife wrote about the event :

Today is the seventh day of J.P.'s . . . preparation for the fast. He is getting used to living on liquids. Milk and milk-based foods are not permitted. He is given two cups of Horlicks, fruit juice and vegetable extracts. But he also exercises, bathes and is given a massage . . . .

. . . Tomorrow J.P. begins his fast. He is very pleased. I do not doubt that he will be able to go through it, and emerge greatly strengthened . . . .

. . . Today is the second day of the fast. Many of J.P.'s closest friends visited him, and despite the doctor's orders, they talked for too long. As a result, J.P. was completely worn out by the evening . . . .

Prabhavatiji too kept a record of this period : 'Today, the twelfth day of the fast, has gone well. Last night, just before he went to sleep, his stomach was troubling him. He had to go to the bathroom three times. Later, the pain eased and he went to sleep, and slept soundly through the night. This morning, after his bath and *maalish* he slept for an hour. He has drunk a lot of water today, and his urine is clear. I do not think he will be nauseous today. . .no signs so far . . . .'

About the sixteenth day of the fast, Mahavir Prasad wrote :

Today is the sixteenth day of the fast. It is amazing, he looks even fresher than he did at the beginning. He has had no nausea or any other complications. At night, his back pains him—he has been a patient of sciatica for many years. Yesterday, a plaster was put on his back, and the pain has eased. Everyday he loses about a pound in weight. He is weak. . . .

Prabhavatiji wrote about the sixteenth day thus :

The sixteenth day . . . . is nearly over. He now weighs 127 pounds. He did not sleep well last night, and he looks somewhat tired. . . .

When the fast was over, she wrote :

J.P.'s health is slowly improving. Today, he has put on one pound, and is getting his strength back. Today he has had the strength to walk on his own. Until yesterday, he had to be carried on a chair. He has slept well . . . .

It took J.P. five months to recoup his health. But in fasting he had found an inner strength, and a vision of the way ahead.

Having spent the whole of the hot season in Poona, J.P. returned to Patna. On the 1st of December, 1951 he explained the reason for his fast to some friends :

Fasting, particularly as a means of self-culture, has had no place in socialist philosophy or practice. I therefore owe a word of explanation.

The fast developed . . . more and more into a self-purificatory sacrifice, and each day brought new inner strength and sometimes an unanticipated experience. I was chary at the beginning of claiming to do anything by way of self-purification. So full of faults and vice one found oneself that it seemed presumptuous to speak, publicly at any rate, of self-purification . . . . Traditionally, socialism has rested on institutional changes for curing the evils of modern society. We have in our movement, however, realised that institutional changes are not enough and that individual man, the root of society, must also be cured. That is why we have latterly been laying more and more emphasis on values and the right means. I am afraid, however, that the aware-

ness of this vital principle has not gone deep enough and
we have not applied it fully to our individual selves.   The
detachment, the self-control, the conquest over desire that
are necessary for us workers are absent in us in ample
measure.   If we have to serve socialism and create a new
society and a new man (which is more important), we must
make ourselves worthy instruments . . . .

Later in the month, J.P. visited Pandol vi!lage and addressed
a public meeting on the subject of voluntary re-distribution of
land. The campaign had been called a *satyagraha*, and J.P.
toured through Sagarpur, Brahmotra, Sohrai, Mandol and
Nokoda villages, addressing the people, and visiting the
families of those satyagrahis who had gone to jail.

J.P. wrote: 'This fast has been for me a cleansing experience.
I claim no more than that and I think it could not have done
any harm to the party. . . .each day brought new inner strength
and sometimes an unanticipated experience.

Two years later, J.P. would perform *jeevan dan*. But the
turning point, the dividing line between the darkness of party
politics and the light of Sarvodaya came somewhere at this
point of time.

Chapter Six

Unswervingly your purpose holds my love,
This role you've set I am content to play;
But now a different drama takes the scene:
Spare me this once the treading of your way.

And yet the order of the acts is planned,
The way's end destinate and unconcealed.
Alone. Now is the time of Pharisees.
To live is not like walking through a field.

—BORIS PASTERNAK

J.P. emerged from darkness into light. What had happened ?
Only two small events : the fast in Poona, and Vinoba's
bhoodan campaign. And yet they had shaken J.P.'s convictions,
his confidence in the intellectual validity of scientific socialism as he had conceived it hitherto. J.P. had seen the light,
some kind of light, but it entailed no sudden, bewildering
change of course. In 1953, J.P. continued to be enmeshed in
Party affairs.

In February that year, Nehru sent forth feelers for some
kind of alliance with the Socialist Party. On behalf of the
Party, J.P. conferred with Nehru in Delhi. The prospect of
office, however, held no allurement for him (J.P.). He made it
clear that he was not interested in joining the Government

unless he was assured that it would move swiftly in the direction of socialism.

On his way to Gaya by train in March 1953 J.P. drafted a
long letter to Nehru, explaining his views at length :

. . . a great deal would depend on how you conceived
your own move in asking for our co-operation. If it means
only this that a few of us are to be added to your cabinet
and some of the State cabinets to strengthen the Government and your hands in carrying out your present policies,
the attempt would not be worth making. But if it means
launching upon a bold joint venture of national reconstruction, it might well have been a historic move . . .

J.P. went on to describe the development of his political
philosophy: 'I assure you our approach to socialism is not doct-
rinaire, tradition-bound or conservative. But I must make one
point clear. No matter how empirical and experimental may
be our approach, the goals and values of socialism are
unalterably fixed before us. Whether we give it or not the
name of any ism, we all desire without the shadow of any
doubt to create a new society in which there is no exploitation, in which there is economic and social equality, in which
there is freedom and well-being for all.'

He added, 'We have all been deeply influenced by Gandhiji.
I do not mind saying that I have been rediscovering him. I
believe he was one of the most vital thinkers of the modern
age . . . . I feel sure that the Gandhians and the socialists,
dropping their respective jargons, must work together.'

In the same letter, J.P. suggested a minimum programme
based on certain constitutional, legal, administrative, fiscal
and economic reforms, agreement to which might furnish
concrete ground for Congress-P.S.P. entente.

J.P.'s letter produced no results—Nehru protested that the
Government was not in a position to implement the 14-point
programme which the P.S.P. wanted, and the P.S.P. did not
agree without a tangible commitment to a programme. Nehru's
ballon d'essai came down—the merger proposal was dropped.
The proceedings, however, led to unsavoury gossip in the
P.S.P. circles, that J.P. had initiated the talk about a merger,
and was secretly wanting to enter the Congress. A lot of
bitterness was stirred up in the Party, and J.P.'s disillusion-

ment came to the surface.

In 1954, another sore burst. The Socialists and members of
the erstwhile Kisan Mazdoor Praja Party, who had joined the
ranks, began to exchange bitter recriminations. The spectacle
of a political organisation having failed at the polls, venting
its frustrations in personal jealousies and taunts, usually
presages the end of its effectiveness. J.P. seemed to withdraw
from the scene in disgust.

In March 1953, J.P. accompanied Vinoba to Gaya. It is
probably true to say that at this point, he was somewhat
sceptical of voluntary land-gifts. But the experience of *bhoodan*
on this visit dispelled all doubts from his mind.

Not only did he begin to see *bhoodan* as a practical solution
to the land problem, J.P. accepted the philosophy of
ahimsa which underlay the movement. In his speeches of the
time, he dissected the failure of socialist revolutions in other
parts of the world. He had come to the conclusion that
violence distorts the revolutionary intention, and leads to
failure. Slowly, inexorably, J.P. was being ushered towards
full-blown Gandhism.

The *bhoodan* campaign picked up momentum and generated
hope and enthusiasm as it swept through the villages. At the
Chandol Sarvodaya Sammelan, Vinoba expounded his concept
of *lok shakti* (the people's power). J.P. became completely captivated by the movement, and he talked animatedly
to crowds of people about Gandhi's vision of self-governing
village republics. For students and the younger generation of
political workers, there was a magic in J.P.'s style of argument, and they came forward eagerly to contribute their mite.

However, J.P. had not yet severed his ties with the P.S.P.,
and he did not neglect party work. There was no contradiction in this double allegiance, for J.P. saw *bhoodan* as an
effective and pure striving after socialism. He had given up
the notion of violence—but the ideal of a socialistic society
remained—only the means were being forged anew.

In April 1954, the sleepy district capital of Bodh Gaya
became the venue of the sixth Sarvodaya Conference under
the leadership of Vinoba. In attendance were Prime Minister
Nehru, Dr. Rajendra Prasad, Dr. Radhakrishnan, Acharya
Kripalani and many other political notables. On the afternoon

of the second day (19th April 1954) J.P. rose to make a
dramatic declaration : he made an offer of his life, a *jeevandan*. Henceforth, he would dedicate his life to the *bhoodan*
movement, and would retire from politics.

In the rest of his address, J.P. called upon young people
and students to help make the movement a success. In Bihar
the movement had not yet attained its target of gifted land,
because of a shortage of workers. Thirty two lakh acres of
land had been given up by landowners, and the Bihar Congress Committee and Bihar P.S.P. had both helped to achieve
this, though they had not co-ordinated their efforts. He called
on all people, irrespective of party affiliation, to bury their
differences to work for a cause that was above political
identity. At the end of his speech, he repeated his pledge of
jeevan dan, and added: 'I am not resigning from the P.S.P.,
but from now I will be only an ordinary member of the
Party . . .'

The next day, Vinoba sent J.P. a letter pledging that he too
would re-dedicate his life to *bhoodan*, the uplift of the villager
and the non-violent revolution.

For Prabhavatiji this was a moment of tremendous happi-
ness. Her only regret was that Bapu was not alive to see
J.P.'s 'conversion'.

When J.P. returned to Patna, he published in the *Janata* a
short explanation of his pledge :

 . . . the decision which I took was not made on the
 spur of the moment. I was being slowly driven towards it
 for months past. Nor did the step signify repudiation of the
 ideals for which I had stood so long. It meant, rather, that
 I had realised that those ideals could be achieved and
 preserved better through *bhoodan* or the Gandhian way . . .

 What do we see in *bhoodan* to be so moved ? To super-
 ficial observers *bhoodan* is just an agrarian reform movement,
 which at best, is preparing the ground for legislation. To
 those who have looked deep, it is a far more significant
 movement. It is the beginning of an all-round social and
 human revolution: human also, because it aims at changing
 man along with society. It is an application on a general
 scale of Mahatma Gandhi's non-violent technique of revolution. In the words of Pyarelalji, 'it is the spearhead of a

non-violent revolution whose implications reach far and wide . . . '

. . . the *jeevandani* who dedicates his life to human and social betterment, must begin by bettering himself. The *jeevandani* is an ordinary mortal with the faults and foibles of his fellow men. But the fact that he has vowed to devote his life to the remaking of men and society means that he has to begin with remaking himself. *Jeevandan* thus becomes a spiritual pilgrimage. For me at least this is its most valuable significance.

Soon after the Conference, J.P. travelled deep into the hilly, forested areas of Gaya district, and established a Sarvodaya *ashram* in a backward village called Sokhodevara. Many years earlier, during the nationalist struggle, the village had been a stronghold of the peasant movement. Now it hosted an *ashram* for the revolution of love.

Sokhodevara is approached through a treacherous route that winds through uncultivated jungle and disappears where the land is bisected by small rivulets and storm-drains. During the rainy season, Sokhodevara is almost completely cut off from the outside world. Despite the daunting route, however, Sokhodevara gradually became a central establishment for workers in the movement. Students who decided to join the movement travelled to Sokhodevara and were trained in the *ashram*. Activists from the P.S.P. and other political parties also journeyed to this remote village and lived at the *ashram*.

The beginnings of the *ashram* were unpretentious. Land was reclaimed from the surrounding jungle, and a few huts were hastily put up. J.P. moved into one of the huts after Prabha had made it livable. More than anyone else, Prabha-ji, affectionately called *didi* by the little community, was responsible for infusing life into the *ashram*. She was there whenever there was work to do—stoking a cooking fire, welcoming guests, looking after the sick, leading the daily prayers, and spinning her *charkha*. Apart from this heavy round of duties, she looked after J.P.'s personal needs, cooked his food, washed his clothes. J.P. was afflicted with diabetes at this time, and Prabhavati even gave him his daily injections of insulin.

Gradually, the *ashram* took shape. J.P.'s work for *bhoodan* took him on extensive tours of the countryside, but his head-quarters were now established at Sokhodevara. His day was always packed with activity. Morning and evening there was a prayer session, the morning prayer followed by *shramdan*. Then there were spinning, discussion groups with Sarvodaya workers, and searching question-answer sessions with visitors to the *ashram*.

Initially, J.P. let it be known that he was still available for consultation to the Party, and continued to devote a considerable amount of time to attending the P.S.P. committees. In October 1954, however, J.P. seemed to have decided to cut down on his party commitments.

On the 3rd January, 1955, J.P. and Prabhavati went on fast together. All day they spun the *charkha*, and it was first time in their lives that they prayed together.

The same month, Vinoba completed his *yatra* in Bihar and moved on to fresh pastures in West Bengal. J.P. parted from Vinoba with great emotion.

Knowing that Vinoba was no longer looking after one part of Bihar, J.P. shouldered the additional burden of being the guiding spirit behind *bhoodan* in the State. His own *yatras* became more frequent, the organisational work at the *ashram* more intense. About this time, J.P. became a vegetarian. His health still troubled him, the diabetes had not subsided. But Prabha was with him, administrating to every need.

Nirmala Deshpande tells a story about one of J.P.'s tours in Gaya :

From Benares, I went to meet him, and found him in a tumble-down school building, reading a book in a dilapidated chair. I looked around for Didi. Sounding peeved, J.P. said : "Nirmala, I had a quarrel with Prabha today, and she has not come with me." I did not say anything; it was 1.30, and lunch had not yet been served. J.P. turned around to someone behind him and angrily demanded to know when the food would arrive. One of the workers said in the Bihari manner : "Immediately, immediately", at which J.P. grew angrier : "For the last

four hours you have been saying 'immediately' " . . . The
man ran off in the direction of the kitchen, but it was not
for another hour or so that the food was brought out in dirty
brass *thalis*. Seeing the food—a mountain of rice, *dal* and
potatoes barely cooked, J.P. was even more upset. In the
afternoon J.P. was served tea in a cracked cup—the tea
was sickly sweet and very strongly brewed. J.P. had one
sip, screwed up his face and pushed his cup away. He
then asked for his file of letters, and was told that it was in
a box which had been left behind at Gaya.

In the evening, an exasperated J.P. sent word to 'Didi'
that she should bring all their luggage and come. An
hour later, she arrived by jeep, and set about unpacking,
organising, as was her wont. "Look Nirmala Bahan", she
said to me, "this is the luggage that J.P. got upset
about. He had told me that I carry too many things,
but all this is for him. I can live out of a small handbag.
Do you think this tea set is for me ? I don't even drink
tea ! He is the one who is fussy." J.P. had walked into
the room and was listening to her talking. He smiled and
said nothing.

1955 was a bad year for the Socialists. The recriminations
and tensions of the last two or three years finally led to a
split in the P.S.P., and the S.S.P. was born as a splinter
group under Dr. Lohia's leadership.

Whatever political ties J.P. still had with the P.S.P. were
now further slackened. His disillusionment with politics at
the electoral level was very nearly complete. Early in 1956,
Acharya Narendra Dev died, and J.P.'s closest tie with the
Socialists snapped.

In April 1958, J.P. and Prabhavati were invited to tour
Europe as guests of the various socialist and pacifist organisations in a number of countries. Two years earlier, at the
Asian Countries' Socialist Conference, J.P. had presented
Sarvodaya as the 'true' road to socialism. Delegates from a
few Western countries, who were present at the Conference
carried home news of the Indian 'experiment' and an advance
wave of interest preceded J.P. on his tour in 1958.

J.P. returned to India in September 1958 and addressed a meeting of the Constitution Club and the Indian Congress for Cultural Freedom in Delhi, on what he had seen in Europe. 'The world,' he said, 'wants peace. The West is sitting on a pile of gunpowder, and yet the atom bomb continues to be made .... without the involvement of the people, a new society cannot be created. To think that a few leaders at the top can create socialism is nonsense. You cannot *enact* socialism . . . .'

Soon after, J.P. developed his views in a pamphlet entitled *Back to Mahatma Gandhi*. He wrote :

.... Primary problems such as those of food and unemployment have not been solved in 11 years of independence. Partisan politicians do no doubt try to solve this situation by acrimonious verbal warfare, mutual mud-slinging and what is termed as *satyagraha*. The constructive outcome of this is wholly out of proportion to the time and energy expended on this sort of thing .... In India we have made democracy the foundation of the nation's reconstruction. The question, therefore, is how within the framework of democracy the people can be mobilised for action .... The long-distance appeals of the leaders of the nation from their seats of power have failed to move the people. Experience has also shown that the usual game of party politics has failed to interest the people. ....It is also patent that the civil servants and the machinery of administration cannot activise the people. They lack the moral authority, the intimate touch and the missionary zeal that are necessary.

How then can this supreme task be accomplished ? The answer in the fewest possible words is : 'By going back to Mahatma Gandhi'. The leader of the country .... must go to the people—to live and work with them, to serve, guide and help them . . . .

In the middle of the year 1959, China invaded Tibet. J.P. felt compelled to condemn this act of aggression by a communist State in the most uncompromising terms. In Calcutta, and then in Madras, speaking at successive conferences on Tibet, he raised the question of human rights. Alluding to the prevarication in the official Indian attitude to events in Tibet, he said, 'The Chinese need our friendship as much as we need theirs. But if the price of friendship is duplicity and condonation of wrong, we must have the courage and honesty to refuse to pay the price. . . .'

In July, 1959 J.P. returned to Sokhodevara once again. His real 'roots', his real purpose were in the vast rural spaces of Bihar. During this respite from his round of speeches and public statements, J.P. drafted his essay on *The Reconstruction of the Indian Polity*. He began by rejecting the theory of democracy as it was practised in the West, and analysed the practice of the Indian party system as it then existed. The people, he concluded, were treated as pawns in the electoral game. But the real villain of the piece was not the Party, but the constitutional democracy, which in fact was premised on the operation of powerful Parties. In its place, J.P. advocated a democratic system that involved the people in its functioning and rejected Parties as hindrances to such participation. This was J.P.'s formulation of partyless democracy which he set out in the aforesaid rigorously argued pamphlet.

J.P.'s *jeevandan* was thus not merely a prostration to an abstract ideal—he had, by now, sketched the blueprint of a Stateless society. He now offered his life to a concrete programme of action.

J.P. has said : 'People have wondered at the strange course of my life; they have said that I have wasted so many years wandering in darkness, but when I reflect in my development, I see an unbroken line of progress. It is true, of course, that I was searching for a way, but it was not a mere groping in the dark . . . .I have no regrets that I have arrived at this point by the path I took. . . .'

From our vantage point in time, it is easy to see how J.P.'s various commitments have all contributed towards his present situation. Scientific Marxism, Gandhi's and Vinoba's spiritualism led him to the cross-roads. His own abiding interest in the social roots of discontent then ushered him towards Sarvodaya, and he has built and expanded on the original conception by drawing from his own revolutionary and political experience. This experience has pointed towards the village as the unit of social process, towards democracy as the self-help and self-rule.

Was this so different from what J.P. had been saying many years ago ? In 1946, in his third letter to Fighters for Freedom, he had written: 'The ultimate object. . .is to establish *gramraj*. A *gramraj* is a self-governing village, a village republic, not merely a Panchayat. This *gramraj* is to be built up by the villagers themselves, by their own initiative and not by the governmental agencies. These would make foreign rule unnecessary, they would become centres of struggle and resistance during a revolution and would constitute the bricks with which the structure of the free Indian Republic could be built . . .' The nucleus of Sarvodaya was already present in J.P.'s ideas a decade before he performed *jeevandan*.

Twelve years after Independence, Prime Minister Nehru re-activated Gandhiji's scheme of *panchayati raj*. The setting up of Panchayats at the village level as decision-making bodies had been envisaged in 1948. Now, with the Congress prestige hinging on the success of the Five-Year Plans, the Government saw the Panchayats as potential developmental organs. A high-level committee was appointed to go into the feasibility of *panchayati raj*, and the green signal was quickly given by the committee. The impetus behind *panchayati raj*, thus had little in common with Gandhiji's original conception. Nehru wanted the Panchayats because they would extend the loaves and fishes of office to the lowest rungs of the populace, and act as agencies for the mobilisation of popular support. Disregarding the motive behind the scheme, J.P. urged that the Sarvodaya movement should extend its cooperation to the Government for the growth of Panchayats. For his part, J.P. spared no effort in urging the rural population to adopt the scheme as quickly as possible.

There remained, however, a huge gap between the official scheme of *panchayati raj* and J.P.'s ideal of *gramraj*. The Government saw the village Panchayat, Panchayat Samitis and *zila parishads* as extensions of its coercive organs at the grass-roots level. Thus, it was not a move towards de-centralisation, but a method of binding the unstructured, unarticulated sections of the people, and making them more amenable to governmental control. Far from wanting to grant the village a sphere of autonomy, the Government attempted to extend its influence by allowing the State to percolate into the basic institutions of the common man. Power was not shared, it had been delegated, and its exercise was subjected to a hierarchy of command from the village upwards.

J.P. supported the scheme on very different assumptions. As he had reiterated so often, the villages would be the 'building blocks' of a democratic society, with the small community providing the basic institutions of the Government. As the character of the Government reforms became clear, J.P. was sorely disappointed.

Early in 1961, J.P. refined his ideas on participatory democracy. In India, a mere grafting of Western democratic institution, he said, resulted in a bias of the State structure in favour of the elite. The 'pyramid', instead of being broad-based, rested on its apex, resulting in a polity both unstable and unjust. The mere fact of universal adult franchise did not confer power to the illiterate masses. Open to manipulation and suggestion, they served to legitimise power, though they remained uninvolved and unincluded in the processes of government. Government, he stressed, would not percolate into the villages—it had to emanate from India's masses.

On the 12th of October, 1962, the Chinese troops invaded NEFA, and at a number of points on the Sino-Indian border, transgressed on Indian territory. Brushing aside the resistance of Indian troops, China occupied Aksai Chin in Ladakh. And just as suddenly as the hostilities began, they ceased.

J.P. made this statement on these events :

We have to answer the challenge. I have said that on the level of the State, the only answer is Democratic Socialism. Pandit Nehru has said that even in an emergency, we will not abandon socialism. But our progress towards this ideal is painfully slow so as to be almost invisible. The people must be involved in this constructive task, and their object must be Sarvodaya. Sarvodaya strives for self-governing socialism or self-governing communism. It is a 'people's socialism' or a 'people's communism', not a State founded on force or on legal compulsion. Today, the nation has rallied to the defence of the country. It is a good sign. The history of society demonstrates that as long internal and external threats were met by concerted action, they continued to develop; as soon as this response by the people atrophied, the society disintegrated. If the challenge of Chinese aggression is not met today, India will disintegrate. The country must be strengthened, but I do not refer to military strength. The only strength can be strength through Sarvodaya. It is the only answer to totalitarian communism...

1963 was an important year for the Sarvodaya movement. In August, Vinoba suggested that the Bihar Sarvodaya Council should dissolve itself in view of its over-institutionalisation. In early September, the Council was dissolved, and J.P. reiterated the call for a Shanti Sena—the movement, aimed to recruit 75,000 volunteers, one soldier of peace for every area with a population of five thousand.

Later that year, in November, the Sarva Seva Sangha met in conference at Arambagh, to commemorate 12 years of the Sarvodaya movement. Traditionally, these annual sessions were a stock-taking of the successes and failures of the movement. J.P. said : 'If the people can solve their problems among themselves and broaden and develop their lives, there will be no need of a Sarva Seva Sangh, a political party or the apparatus of the State. The ultimate aim of our movement is to bring about such a situation, where the people can help themselves without the intervention of political organisations.'

It was at the Arambagh session that J.P. decided against expanding his efforts on a nationwide campaign, and to concentrate instead on some small, precise field of operations. For this purpose, J.P. chose Gaya, Purnea and the Santhal Pargana as his special field of work.

The last years of Nehru's life were burdened as much by the weight of adverse events as by a mood of pessimism. Nehru's health declined, and the question, 'After Nehru, who ?' was whispered on street corners. Only nine months before his death, the Congress had shrunk back from the thought of his resigning under the Kamaraj Plan. Gloom about India's wayward foreign policy and the internal rot had permeated to the very roots of political life. It was, above all, a time of uncertainty.

In May 1964 J.P. had become involved with the Naga hostiles who had been raiding Government check-posts

across the border in East India. As a member of the Peace
Mission, and accompanied by Michael Scott, J.P. travelled to
NEFA and met with secessionist tribal chieftains. It was two
weeks later, when J.P. returned to Calcutta that he heard of
Pandit Nehru's death on the afternoon of May 27. He was
moved to tears despite the vicissitudes of their political relationship: 'Today the captain of the ship is no more. The
leader of the Indian people has left them bereft and gone. If
we want to steer the ship of State safely through these turbulent waters, and remain true to our departed leader, we
have now to work with courage and discipline, to work
shoulder to shoulder and face the challenge.'...J.P. was moved
to tears when he read Nehru's last will and testament.

The Fourth General Elections were scheduled for 1967.
The political firmament was in a flux, and J.P. called for a
partyless democracy that would deal with urgent problems
without rancour and ideology.

The Congress Party suffered a serious setback in the
General Elections. Although its share of the total votes polled
did not seriously decline, its share of Parliamentary seats
declined from 73% (in 1962) to 55% and in the Vidhan
Sabhas from 62% to 51%. The Congress Ministries in a
number of States were ousted by the Opposition or United
Front Ministries.

Meanwhile, J.P. launched his movement for Bihar-*dan* in
late 1968. The biggest district of Bihar, Darbhanga, had
already been offered as *zila-dan*, with more than three-fourths
of its land voluntarily given up to the Sarvodaya movement.
It seemed as though the time had come for Sarvodaya to
move from the village and district to the level of the whole
State. A new era in the history of *bhoodan* was begun.

In June 1970, J.P. was in ill-health, and convalescing in the
hills at a little station called Pauri in Garhwal. Suddenly, he
received a letter saying that two officials of the district
Sarvodaya Mandal had been threatened with their lives by
a group of Naxalites in Muzaffarpur. According to the letter,
the two officials—Badri Narayan Singh and Gopal Mishra—
would be assassinated on the 5th and 7th of June respectively.
    J.P. rushed to Muzaffarpur, and announced his intention

of staying at Musehari, where Naxalite activists were known to be operating. This was on June 3. The next task was to locate the two men whom the Naxalites had threatened to shoot. One of them was found in Muzaffarpur. The other was located 22 miles out of the town, in a village.

On June 4, J.P. began a string of conferences and speeches at which he explained the situation to the people. The whole area had been panic-stricken for some months. The Naxalites' method of execution had followed a pattern of warning the person by letter, appointing a day, and then shooting him. There had been a number of armed robberies. The police had been powerless to suppress the Naxalites, and the villagers were paralysed with fear.

On June 8, J.P. addressed a big public meeting in Muzffarpur: 'Let no one here think that we have spent all our arrows. The Sarvodaya movement has completed its first objectives of *satyagraha* and of educating the people in our methods. Now we are going to launch the second phase of the movement—to complete our programme, to strengthen its roots, we will launch another *satyagraha*. From tomorrow, Prabhavati and myself will walk to every village in Musehari. We will come to your doors and we will explain. If necessary, we will go without food and offer *dharna* and we will insist that if you want to feed us, then you must make arrangements to see that the hungry people in your villages do not go without food. You must give them one twentieth of your land . . . .' Referring to the threat to kill the Sarvodaya officials, he said, 'Do not think that we are afraid of threats or the danger to our lives. We move through the villages. It is easy for anyone to kill us while we are engaged in our work. Despite all the security arrangements, if Gandhi and Kennedy could be assassinated, how can ordinary men like us escape from an assassin's bullet ?. . . We are not at all worried by the thought of death. As long as God protects us, we will live, when He chooses that we should die, we will die . . . . !

Thereafter, J.P. and Prabhavati began their tour of Musehari. To the downcast, disheartened Sarvodaya workers, this was a beacon of courage. J.P. and Prabhavati were joined by an eager band of Sarvodaya workers. Before they set out, J.P. issued a manifesto explaining the nature of their aims:

The Naxalite problem really poses the question of whether or not peaceful solutions can be found to air social, economic and political ills. I would like your co-operation in understanding and tackling this problem because they (the Naxalites) are equally products of these conditions. Every political party attempts to tackle these conditions in its own way. Some of these efforts must be apparent to you. But you must not believe that this is only a task for outside agencies. You, too, must contribute, and as far as your methods are democratic and just, I will support you.

The programme of Sarvodaya is above Party affiliation. We are neither for nor against any particular Party. We desire a polity without Parties. The ideals of Sarvodaya are close to those of socialism and communism, though we stress the independence and power of the common people— we stress the decentralisation of economic and political power so that it resides in collective organisations of the people.

Sarvodaya strives to attain its ends through the people, through *lok shakti*. In this respect, it is similar to violent revolution, because neither of them is brought about through processes of law. A violent revolution too must base itself in the support of the people. The difference, however, is that a violent revolution succeeds after great efforts in wiping out the old society, and then being another long effort to try and establish a new society. A non-violent revolution, on the other hand, accomplishes these tasks simultaneously—the changing of the old order, and the shaping of the new, take place together.

The first camp on J.P.'s itinerant mission was held on the premises of the middle school at Salha village, nine miles away from Muzaffarpur. At this first *sabha*, J.P. addressed the assembled villagers on the subject of peace and non-violence. 'If you want to prevent this country from slipping into war and violence, then you have to tread the way that Gandhiji and Vinobaji have indicated. It will not be easy. . . .' The villagers, uncomprehending and benumbed with fright, left the assembly confused, and full of doubts. Was J.P. really trying to protect the rich against the violence of the poor ? They wondered.

J.P., accompanied by Prabhavati and a band of supporters, began his campaign for a peaceful revolution in Musehari. He was determined to demonstrate to the Naxalites that there was an alternative to their method of assassination and violence. The work progressed slowly at first: the villagers were not used to J.P.'s style of engaging them in argument. Gradually, however, their suspicions were stilled, they learned to trust J.P. and genuine enthusiasm was kindled.

J.P. and his small band of followers visited every village in Salha Panchayat. He talked to every villager he met, big or small—there was no sudden enlightenment, but there was a visible relaxing of tensions, the way for a dialogue had been opened. The mood of suspicion and fear was disappearing, and the villagers warmed to the idea of forming village communities to resolve their problems. The notion of self-government took root.

From Salha, J.P. moved to Prahladpur. Here again, a meeting in every village was held—meetings, discussions, grievances, arguments. He visited the families of the victims of the Naxalites, and the families whose members were reported to be Naxalites.

On 18th April 1971, the first campaign in Musehari was completed, and a mammoth rally to commemorate *Bhoodan* Day was organised. Hundreds of thousands of flag-waving, poster-bearing, slogan-shouting villagers from all over Musehari converged at the meeting-ground. J.P. reminded the crowds about the lessons of the past year: 'If these men are not mere dacoits and murderers parading as revolutionaries, then I want to tell them that what will emerge from their revolution is not a new man, but a demon. And they will be responsible for bringing about a dehumanised civilisation. . . .'

Musehari was the supreme test of Sarvodaya—for J.P. it was a trial by ordeal, where, for the first time, the passions of violence confronted the forces of peace and persuasion. The miracle was that J.P. had emerged unscathed, and the villagers fired with a new enthusiasm in the exercise of self-rule. An extract from one of J.P.'s articles of the time sums up the efforts made by him :

Our experiences in the four months and more that we have been here have been quite varied, and on the whole interesting and encouraging. At first we took one Panchayat at a time and concentrated on its villages. Usually there are 4 to 7 revenue villages in a Panchayat, whose average population works out to about 7,000 each, some being smaller, some larger. As the number of our workers increased, we started to spread out and take two, even three, Panchayats at a time. So far we have been spending from 15 to 20 days in a Panchayat before moving on to the next. But we always leave behind one worker or more to complete the work there.

The villages in this area—I am sure it is not much different elsewhere in this State—are in a deplorable state, both morally and materially. Poverty and backwardness are only too obvious. Equally obvious are the near collapse of community life and the absence of any sense of belonging. The communities are rent with feuds and factions, with the attendant litigation, tensions, and moral chaos. The usual phenomena of social and economic disparities, of exploitation, injustice and oppression are, needless to say, obtrusively present everywhere. It is clear that if something is not done soon to pull the villages out of this morass, they will sink deeper into it, dragging the whole country down with them, as seems to be happening already to this State.

In such a situation, it is natural that our presence here should be looked upon by the people as an annoying intrusion into their accustomed ways of life. But it also happens that in every Panchayat there are one or more persons who give us a welcome and come forward to help us. And as time passes, and we persist patiently in our mission, the climate slowly changes and the people begin to respond. As a rule, the landless labourers are the first to respond, then the small farmers. Gradually the middle farmers come over, and a time comes when the resistance of the bigger farmers too begins to break. What seems to stick in their throats are : (a) renouncing their proprietary title to their land; and (b) joining the direct democracy of the *gram sabha*. Their feudal and upper-caste mentality

inhibits them from reconciling themselves to the political
equality of the *sabha*. They fear the overwhelming majority
of the poor, even though they are assured that decisions
can be taken only by unanimity or consensus. The money-
lenders are the last to change. There are, of course, ex-
ceptions to this general pattern.

. . .As our aim is not to divide the community and set one
part against the other but to integrate it, we are seeking to
create community consciousness and a sense of mutual
responsibility, and are trying to bring together the different
conflicting interests, that are really interdependent, into
mutual confrontation in the village parliament so as to
set in motion a process of resolution of conflicts and
problems by mutual adjustment that will lead to a juster
and better social order. Thus, ours is not a trade union
but a community approach . . .

Some critics say that the *Gramdan* movement does not
go far enough. Of course, that is true, if they are measuring the distance from the ultimate goal. But what does go
far enough ? I have already dwelt upon the question of the
time that a violent revolution takes to reach the ultimate
goal. I know of none that has reached it irrespective of
the time taken. As for the legal method, it is not realised
that in many respects *gramdan* goes farther than the law
has done until now or can do in the future. It all depends
on what your goal is. If it is transformation—even though
national and formal in law—of individual ownership into
community ownership of land; if it is establishment of a
participatory village democracy; if it is inculcation of the
spirit of self-reliance and co-operative endeavour among
the rural people—if it is all this, the law simply cannot
achieve it. Even in the matter of re-distribution of land,
one-twentieth part certainly seems to be very little. But it
should be borne in mind that: (*a*) this applies even to those
whose holdings are below the ceiling, and would still apply
even if the ceiling were drastically reduced, and (*b*) that so
far the ceiling law has not yielded, at least in this State,
a single surplus cent of land for redistribution. And it is
not that the Congress Party alone has been in power all
these years—all the major parties in the State, not to speak

of the minor ones, have had their hand on the steering
wheel of the State. Moreover, let it not be forgotten that
gramdan is not the consummation of Sarvodaya; it is only
a step towards it. Other steps are to follow.

In October 1971 a tall hefty man visited J.P. at his home in
Kadam Kuan, Patna. He introduced himself as Ram Singh,
a jungle *thekedar* from the Chambal ravines, and claimed that
he had been sent by the dacoits of that region. 'I have come',
he told J.P 'because the dacoits of the Chambal valley want
to surrender to you.'

J.P. was surprised, but asked him to go to Vinoba. The
man persisted. 'Listen to me, Babuji, I am not speaking about
10 or 20 *dakoos*. All the *dakoos* of that region will surrender,
there will be no more *dakoos*. . . .Vinobaji has asked me to
see you. My real name is Madho Singh."

J.P. was thunderstruck. Madho Singh ! 'There is a reward
of one and a half lakhs for your arrest ! Why have you come
to me ?' he asked.

'We trust you. That is why I have come.'

J.P. did not know what to say. Madho Singh prostrated
himself at J.P.'s feet and became the first dacoit to surrender.
J.P. made arrangements for Madho Singh to stay with him,
and told Prabhavati, but no one else.

Then began a round of feverish messages to the Central
Home Minister, and the Chief Ministers of Madhya Pradesh,
U.P. and Rajasthan. In 1960, Vinoba had sent a Peace
Mission to the Chambal valley, and J.P. summoned its workers,
Mahavir Bhai and Hemdev Sharma, to Patna for consultation.
A new Peace Force was organised, and Mahavir Bhai and
Hemdevji were asked to handpick a group of workers for
their task. The Mission quickly recruited the services of
Charan Singh and Pandit Lokman (the erstwhile notorious
dacoit Lukka).

J.P. fell ill at the beginning of November that year, as a
result of the cumulative strain of the past two years. The
doctors feared that he had suffered a mild heart-attack, but
fortunately, this proved baseless. Nevertheless, for three
months, J.P. was incapacitated, and spent this period in complete rest. The work of the Peace Mission went on.

Thousands of leaflets comprising this appeal were scattered in the valley. Madho Singh, acting on behalf of the dacoits, asked : 'We are ready to give up our arms. But is society prepared to accept us ?' This was a question aimed, not so much at J.P. or the people, but at the processes of law. All of the month of January 1972, officials of the State and Central Government conferred about the possible implications of waiving the normal course of justice.

Early in February that year, J.P.'s strenuous efforts to get *dakoo* Man Singh's son, Tehsildar Singh, released from jail, bore fruit. He too, was inducted as a member of the Peace Mission, with a jail record of 12 years behind him.

His health restored and the Bangladesh war concluded, J.P. travelled to Delhi in February to pursue his plans. While in Delhi, he received letters from Madho Singh that began 'Dear Pitaji (father)....' On March 1, 1972, Madho Singh came to Delhi with Mahavir and Hemdev. And on April 11, 1972, J.P. left for Gwalior by helicopter, to begin his talks with the dacoits.

At Gwalior, he was met by a host of journalists, policemen, district officials and enthusiastic citizens. Along the way, every little village turned out to cheer J.P.'s jeep, and post signs saying 'Welcome'. J.P. travelled to Morena, then to Jaura Ashram and by a dusty track, on to Pagarkothi. He arrived at five o'clock in the evening and met a group of dacoits, led by Mohar Singh. All of the next day, he talked to the band of men, and on the following day, two well-known dacoits, Makhan Singh and Swaroop Singh, arrived by jeep.

At a public meeting on the evening of April 14 in 1972 at Gandhi Ashram, Jaura, Mohar Singh, Swaroop Singh, Pancham Singh, Tilak Singh, Naresh Singh and their bands (82 men in all) surrendered their arms. On the 16th, another 81 men surrendered, and were followed on the 17th, by Nathu Singh and his men.

Nathu Singh said to J.P. : 'Until today, we only met people who wanted to capture or kill us. You are the only person who has wanted to save us.' Madho Singh spoke to a representative of the B.B.C. 'What is Jayaprakash Babu? He is the light of victory (*jaya-ka-prakash*). The victory of non-violence, love and sympathy.'

Chapter Seven

DURING the *Gramdan* movement, J.P. had asked a group
of educated villagers if they had heard of Trotsky. 'He
talked of a permanent revolution and was assassinated
by Stalin because when the revolutionary succeeds to
power, he is no longer interested in permanent revolution. But
we have created organs which are capable of waging a
permanent revolution—when a village council (*gram sabha*)
is set up, it becomes a potential agency of permanent
revolution. . . .'

But what had happened to this revolution—why did it
always lapse into inertia and complacence, belying the vigour
and idealism that had gone into its making ? Was it true that
'the people' would always remain a passive entity, paying
taxes and homage, and expecting law and order in return ?
Why did 'the people' consistently neglect institutions like the
gramsabha allowing a creative agency of self-government
to atrophy and rot away ? Was India still steeped in the
mediaevalism of *raja-praja*, the king and his subjects ?

J.P. had not lost faith in the possibilities of Sarvodaya
—but he had begun to ask fundamental questions about the
institutionalisation of reform and development. The Welfare
State, as it had emerged in Europe, was undoubtedly an advance in the political philosophy of utilitarianism and *laissez-
faire*. But history had shown that it was a conceptual
advance that had failed to devise the means of attaining its
goals. The Welfare State was mediated by the bureaucracy,

the concept was concretised in impersonal institutions—and in course of time, these institutions had ossified and become divorced from the original intention. Men became numbers, problems became files, human contact vanished, and an encrustation of corruption and selfishness choked the life-blood of institutions of welfare. The Indian experiment with democratic institutions had been particularly tragic, and it had floundered in the particular circumstances of an electoral mandate to centralised bureaucratic rule. Cottage Industries, *panchayati raj*, even *bhoodan* were victims of the political system. The lack of initiative, apathy, burgeoning poverty, were products of the alienation of the Government from the people.

Late in life, J.P. had once more come to the crossroads. A characteristic series of acts, which have preceded every new involvement in J.P.'s life, once again unfolded. Before he plunged into Sarvodaya, his political ties with the P.S.P. first grew slack, and then shaded off into the cathartic fast in Poona. This time, he announced his intention to go into retreat for a year on his 69th birthday. In a letter addressed to all his associates, he wrote :

Today, the 11th of October 1971, I have completed 69 years of my life. If I live until then, I shall be 70 on October 11, 1972. I am writing this to tell you of a personal decision that I have taken, with the full concurrence of my wife, that from October 11, 1972 to October 11, 1973, that is, for that entire period of 12 months, I shall withdraw myself completely from every kind of public and social work and sever my connection with every organisation with which I am connected now, or may become connected in the year following today, October 11, 1971. I shall resign not only from any office that I may be holding in any organisatian or institution on October 10,1972, but also from ordinary or executive membership as the case may be.

What I shall do, if I am still alive, during the period of withdrawal, I do not know. I know only this, that it will be for me a period of complete rest and retreat. I do not presume to give to this period any high-sounding name, such as time of "spiritual renewal", "intellectual re-equipment", or anything so pretentious. For me it will mean nothing more than simply a period of rest. During this period I shall not attend any public function, seminar, organisational/institutional or even "consultative" meeting or get-together. I shall do exactly as the spirit moves me.

Friends can meet me during this period by appointment, but I shall not discuss with them any organisational or institutional matters. Nor shall I give anyone any advice regarding any public question or about policies or programmes af action. Not being in the active field myself, I would consider it wrong of me to offer any advice about such matters.

I may, however, write, and even publish, during this period if I happen to feel like it.

There is only one eventuality in which I might, if I so wished, emerge from my retreat, namely, in the case of a serious national emergency, that is to say, an emergency that appears serious to me and not merely one that the Government of India might declare.

I hope all the organisations and institutions with which I am connected will utilise this one year's notice, given herein, to make any arrangement they may wish in view of my year's withdrawal from 11 October, 1972.

What I shall do after the expiry of the period of retreat, I do not know. I know only this that until body and mind keep functioning, I shall continue to serve my country and the world. I know also that the style of my future work will have to change radically, because the present style has proved too wasteful of time and energy, both physical and mental. More than this I cannot say at present about my future, which really rests in the hands of God.

In the midst of his work for the dacoits of the Chambal valley, J.P. had once more been struck by an attitude of self-analysis. He had not sought the role of the saviour of the dacoits—one of them had approached and surprised him with the offer of surrender, and thereafter events had swept him up of their own accord. In the midst of unexpected success, J.P. was prompted to stop and take stock of his work for Sarvodaya, and he decided that his involvement had prevented him from objectively analysing the efficacy and usefulness of this work. And so, a full year of introspection was carved out of his life ; he would resume his crusade from some uncertain point on his seventieth birthday.

Today, long after this question-mark has been answered by J.P.'s new involvements, it is easy to see the reasons for his restlessness, and to read significance into his utterances at the time. Before his year of rest, pondering over the continual setbacks to *gramdan*, J.P. said :

We have to go to the root of problem, we have been picking at the leaves and branches for too long. Sores have broken out over the whole body, there is no use attending to individual sores. . . .The only remedy is a blood transfusion and a total cure. Violence, fraud, corruption have poisoned the blood of society. We have to remember that all the individual problems of society must be tackled at the roots, at the very foundations of the system. Economic, social and political conditions rest on weak foundations. Without changing these foundations, and adjusting the ideals, we cannot solve anything. And that is why I say, we must get to the root of the problem, otherwise we are wasting our energy. Nothing will be achieved by putting on a show, or by going to jail. We have to work terribly hard, we have to revaluate our choices and purge the infected soil of our society of its poisons. . . .

In his statements of a later date, J.P. elaborated on his critique of the political process. Soon after the elections in 1972, in which there were allegations of widespread corruption and 'ballot-stuffing', J.P. said :

This is not new. These practices have happened before, but it seems now that if democracy is to survive, the electoral system must be completely revamped. . . . Advancing beyond the practices associated with a parliamentary democracy, in particular, party politics, we want to establish a people's government based on a system that functions without Parties—such a state of affairs will be called 'communitarian democracy'.

...The way in which power has been accumulated by the Centre is a matter of grave concern. It is not even that this power has crystallised in central institutions, it has accumulated in the hands of one person. The Congress Party, despite its successes at the polls, has become an empty, meaningless Party. The Congress Chief Ministers are not concerned with the people's good, but with the wishes of the Prime

Minister. In the name of socialism, a totalitarian State has been erected, with all economic power in the hands of the centre, and all its decisions dependent on the personal command of the Prime Minister. The independence of the Press is being steadily whittled away, in the guise of moves to correct the monopolistic control of big industry over the Press. Educational institutions too are completely at the mercy of governmental grants, and the freedom of academic institutions has become a farce.

Gradually, J.P.'s thoughts on a new polity began to take concrete shape—partyless Panchayats at the village level, and partyless politics at the national level alone, he argued, could summon up the necessary incentives to work for the people's good.

At this time tragedy struck. In October 1972, J.P. visited the Benares Medical College hospital to have a carbuncle on his hand treated. The carbuncle was operated upon successfully, but before J.P. left, he insisted that Prabha undergo a routine check-up. It was discovered that she had cancer of the ovary—she must have silently borne the pain, without telling a soul, for many months, if not years, for the sarcoma was in an advanced stage. When questioned about it, Prabha said she had not wanted to interfere with J.P.'s work.

But now, of course, J.P. was sick with worry. He whisked Prabha away to Bombay in November that year, where Dr. Paymaster of the Tata Hospital examined Prabhavati and decided to operate immediately. On the 4th of December 1973, the operation was successfully performed, and six weeks later, J.P. and Prabha left for Calcutta.

It was too much to hope that Prabhavati was rid of the cancerous tissue once and for all. But soon after she arrived at her brother's house at Calcutta, she grew sick again; the pain returned, she began vomiting, and Dr. Paymaster was summoned post haste from Bombay. J.P. was now beside himself with grief and worry, for it had become apparent that Prabha would not recover from this illness.

In the month of February, they returned to Patna, all the while Prabha suffering greater bouts of pain and nausea. Then back to Tata Hospital in Bombay, where the doctors admitted that there was now nothing to be done but to wait for the end.

En route to Patna, Prabhavati met lots of her friends in Delhi for the last time. With a superhuman effort, she continued to conceal her suffering and pain, and once back in Patna, she involved herself in a nephew's wedding as though nothing was the matter. She supervised arrangements, greeted the guests, and participated in the festivities, all the time brushing aside the notion that she was ill and incapacitated. Even on her deathbed, she was a tireless mother to everyone.

During the wedding, she received a letter from Vinobaji that said :

> Dear Prabhavati,
>
> Ram Krishna Hari.

As the end drew close, Prabhavati's frail body was wracked with pain. She moved her bed out of J.P.'s room so that he would not hear her moaning in sleep. Whenever J.P. came into her room, she would act as though she was all right, not wanting to convey any of her dreadful suffering to him.

A few days after they moved house from Kadam Kuan to the wedding house in Gandhi Road. J.P. arranged for a woman from the Kasturba Trust to come and be with Prabhavati. On April 15, 1973, her condition worsened. The marriage ceremonies were hastily concluded—J.P. sat anxiously at Prabha's bedside, watching her agony, wracked by sorrow and sympathy himself. J.P. left the room for a moment to send for a doctor, but when he returned, Prabha had breathed her last with her head in the woman's lap. With her dying breath, she managed to articulate 'Bapu... Baa....'

J.P.'s grief was uncontrollable. In that moment, he was suddenly alone, bereft of the support of a lifetime. But perhaps it is this unfamiliar solitude that has allowed him since Prabhavati's death, to merge with the multitude, to seek refuge from loneliness in the cause.

Early in 1973, Biju Patnaik met J.P. and outlined his plans for a joint front of Opposition parties. J.P. was firm, however, in his view that an anti-Government platform meant nothing by itself. Moreover, he was reluctant to plunge into a political situation which might mirror those conditions which had led him to withdraw from the Socialist Party in 1954.

The same month, J.P. went to Delhi, where he was besieged by the leaders of the Opposition parties. A wave of speculation about his political re-involvement had preceded him to Delhi, but he seemed aloof and unexcited by the idea of leading an anti-Congress movement at the head of the other political groups.

At the end of his talks with politicians of the Opposition, J.P. was convinced that these political parties, more than ever before, lacked an effective programme and direction. Over the years, they had forfeited the people's confidence, and now were desperately scheming to climb back into the public eye. Unity was another matter—how they would eliminate rancorous rivalry and squabbles about precedence was a question to which no answers were available. Was it reasonable to suppose that, at a stroke, they would submerge their identities and ideological differences and close ranks ?

And yet, the situation in India cried out for redress. Spiralling inflation and unempolyment, and a loss of confidence in the Government had prepared the way for new, radical solutions. Was there no way of providing an alternative to a corrupt, complacent, incompetent Government ?

Before she died, Prabha had urged J.P. to do some concentrated writing. She was sceptical about the value of speeches and rousing addresses; people listened and did not retain any of the substance of these speeches. They had become inured to the spoken word, they were subjected to it from every spectrum of the political world, and they had learnt to disregard it irrespective of its value.

Thirteen days after Prabha's death, the last rites completed, J.P. left for Sitab Diyara. It was a sad visit, because he was reminded of the moments in their life together at every turn in the way. At the end of July 1973, J.P. left for Bombay, and revived Gandhi's conception of Trusteeship as a means of settling worker-managerial disputes in industry. Soon after, however, he fell very ill, and was hospitalised for a fortnight. The doctors advised a prolonged rest, and J.P. returned to Patna and then to Sitab Diyara.

His seventy-first birthday found J.P. at Sokhodevra *ashram*.

On this day—11th October, 1972—in terms of his resolution, he was to have winded up activities and retreated into contemplation for a year—with Prabha. . . .

Arrangements for the resettlement of the Chambal valley dacoits, meanwhile, went on. In November 1973, J.P. left Delhi on tour to Bina to inaugurate the Open Jail where the dacoits and their families were to be rehabilitated. Interest in these developments had not abated, and all along the way J.P. was mobbed by an eager press of people. J.P. travelled by festooned train to Mungavali, and then by car to Bina, where he was given a tumultuous welcome. Officials of the Madhya Pradesh Government, the Press corps, and thousands of villagers from all around had gathered together to witness this culmination of a truly unique experiment.

Just beyond the Circuit House, where J.P. was staying, were the tents of the Peace Mission on the right, and on the left, a large awning where it was expected that he would receive the dacoits. Two kilometres away from the Circuit House, a small road led to the Navjivan (meaning New Life) camp and the premises of the open jail. All along this road small welcome gates, made of leaves and flowers, punctuated the progress of the procession. The air was festive rather than solemn, the mood jubilant rather than tentative.

At three in the afternoon, the inaugural ceremonies began. A crowd of seven thousand people was present. A brass band from the Jabalpur Jail, instruments glinting in the sun, and seventy dacoits dressed in khadi, provided the centre of attraction. These men, who had once been the scourge of the Chambal forests, now began to sing *bhajans*. Facing them, on the dais, were large pictures of Gandhi and Vinoba, and sitting in front, were J.P., Chief Minister Sethi and front-ranking officials of the Madhya Pradesh Government and Peace Mission workers. The *bhajans* were followed by a short address by the Minister for Jails, and then, by J.P. This was November 14. The next day J.P. returned to the Navjivan camp and met the dacoits who had already begun to make their homes in the camp. Madho Singh, Mohar Singh and a few other leaders were wearing their old, awesome uniforms, in preparation for the shooting of a short film on their lives by the

Gandhi Film Committee. After a short tour of the premises, J.P. was asked to make a farewell speech. The scene was so reminiscent of the meeting at Pagara a year and a half ago, that J.P. was reminded of Prabha, and his voice choked with emotion.

When the time came for him to leave, Madho Singh touched J.P.'s feet and said : 'Babuji, get well soon. . . and then come back to visit us. . . . Do not worry about us at all. . . . We are converts....'

In the first week of January 1974, J.P. began a new mission for an old cause. At Varanasi (Benares), he addressed a meeting of politically unaffiliated students and sounded his clarion call. 'You must now assume a heavy responsibility,' he told the students. 'Not only you have to protect the existing democratic institutions from crumbling, but you have now to push ahead with the task of implementing Gandhi's vision of *gram-raj* and the self-government of the village community.' J.P. counselled discipline and courage, for such a programme was no longer seen as compatible with the interests of the Congress Party, which would endeavour to obstruct them at every turn. The students had to be careful not to allow the Government to unleash its repressive instruments against such an effort. But if the movement remained true to its ideals of *ahimsa*, then the Government would have no legitimate excuse for violently curbing their efforts.

It was a short, succint address, and J.P. had said many of these things before. But this time, it no longer sounded as though he was merely enunciating a general principle—he was urging the students to struggle, and to action.

That the note of urgency and intent in J.P.'s words was not lost on his audience is clear from the subsequent events in Gujarat, where a powerful student-led movement to disband the State legislature came up.

As the elections to a limited number of State legislatures approached, in February 1974, J.P.'s involvements began to snowball. From Varanasi he travelled to Lucknow, and galloped through a series of meetings with doctors, lawyers, teachers, journalists and students. To all these groups, he urged an active role in seeing that the electoral system was not perverted by the machinations of the Party, or by the role of big money.

In the latter half of January, J.P. returned to Musehari where a number of Sarvodaya workers were still engaged in consolidating the work that was started in 1970. He spent a fortnight touring the villages, supervising the developmental work, seeing that *gram sabhas* were functioning as he had envisaged.

J.P. was back in Delhi in February 1974 where he received representatives of the Sarvodaya group working in Gujarat. Narayan Desai and Kanti Bhai were among the delegates. They told J.P. that the political situation in the State was becoming tense, and that students, intellectuals and a growing number of ordinary people had asked that J.P. visit them at this critical juncture. J.P. cancelled his engagements in Allahabad and Varanasi, and proceeded to Ahmedabad.

The capital city of Ahmedabad was in turmoil. The agitation for dissolution of the Gujarat Assembly had begun, and the Opposition parties, sensing an opportunity for humiliating the Congress Ministry, had joined the struggle. The whole movement, however, threatened to come apart at the seams and spill over into senseless violence for lack of an effective programme or leadership. The students, of course, were in the vanguard, and, at the time when J.P. arrived, were propagating the struggle by going on fast.

J P. stayed five days, utilising this time less to air his own views than to study the rapidly changing situation. He met with and listened to people representing various sections of the townsfolk, and returned to Delhi on the 15th of February. The same day he had a brief talk with Prime Minister Indira Gandhi. Then suddenly, he fell ill and his work slowed.

Nearly a month later, his health somewhat repaired, J.P. travelled to Patna, where on March 18, the offices of the *Searchlight* were burnt down. The next day, he made a statement to the Press:

Anyone with the least sensitivity and patriotism, who was in Patna on the 18th of March (1974) and knew something of what was happening would have found it difficult to withhold his tears. Even as I scribble these lines, tears are welling up. Not only has the *Searchlight*, that beacon of the freedom movement, been destroyed, but much else. It is Bihar's very soul that is torn and bleeding today. I wonder if Bihar will be allowed to be destroyed . . . . In any democratic country, after such a monumental failure of administration as Patna witnessed on Monday last, the Government would have resigned.

He followed this up with another stinging indictment of the Bihar (Congress) Government :

My earnest advice to the Bihar Government is not to deny to the students and the people the right of peaceful protest and action. On the 21st (of March, 1974), a silent procession of the Chhatra Sangharsh Samiti was disallowed and a number of arrests were made. The Bihar Shanti Sena Samiti has been seeking permission to take out a silent procession through the town, but so far the authorities have been evasive. The Chhatra Sangharsh Samiti has not been allowed to hold a public meeting, and at least two arrested students are reported to have been beaten up. If the Government continues to suppress peaceful movements of the people in this manner, there is bound to be a violent explosion. The Government seems to be completely out of touch with the mood of the people.

J.P. then announced that he would march in a silent procession with the Patna *satyagrahis* on April 8. The battle with the Congress Government was joined and Mrs. Indira Gandhi's attitude hardened into bitterness.

In Bhubaneshwar, on the 1st of April Mrs. Gandhi assailed J.P.'s peaceful movement in vitriolic terms : 'It is unfortunate that some people, including certain social workers, have lost interest in village development work and are trying to become politically active. We all know that this kind of peaceful movement is never successful. Their intention has nothing at all to do with the results of this kind of a movement. . . .'

Harsh words ! But there was a certain restraint evident in the oblique references, the sarcasm and the unwillingness to specify names. This restraint did not last long. A few days later, the Prime Minister claimed that Acharya Vinoba had expressed his disapproval of Sarvodaya involvement with the movement. She went on to castigate J.P. by name implying that he got the funds for his movement from dubious sources.

J.P. replied to this diatribe thus :

It does not seem dignified to comment on the kind of remarks Indiraji seems to have made about me in

Bhubaneshwar, yet my silence might be misconstrued in some quarters. My humble submission to Indiraji is not to presume to teach me and other Sarvodaya workers where our duties lie and not to use her proven skill in trying to drive a wedge between me and Vinobaji and thus split the Sarvodaya movement.

There is complete understanding between me and Vinobaji and each of us knows the limits of our agreement and disagreement as of difference in approach to certain problems. There is absolutely no difference in matters of principle. Anyway, it is not for Indiraji but for Vinobaji himself and the Sarva Seva Sangh to guide the Sarvodaya movement. As for Indiraji's remark about those taking money from the rich having no right to talk about corruption, I must say that she is descending to a plane to which I cannot lower myself.

In my article titled *To the Detractors* (*Everyman's*, October 13, 1973) I have frankly explained how I have maintained myself all these years. I have nothing further to add except this . . . If Indiraji's measuring stick were applied universally, Gandhiji would be found to be the most corrupt of all, because his entire entourage was supported by his rich admirers. I wonder how long will the people of this country have to put up with such fantastic nonsense from our high and mighty.

Before Independence, the adulation which Gandhiji was accorded by the Indian people had been a unique phenomenon. Tens of thousands of people surrounded him wherever he went; he was a leader whose following had been without parallel in the modern world. When he died, an age passed away, and the Indian political scene adjusted to smaller men hauling their lesser eminence like long shadows. After the great beacon of the Mahatma, his successors seemed to have the mite of fireflies, flitting in confusion where he himself had blazed a trail.

On the 8th and 9th of April, Patna looked as though Gandhiji had returned. J.P. had promised to march in procession through the city and hundreds of thousands of people had responded to his call. No Indian leader since Gandhiji has been able to call upon the love and allegiance of so many people for a political cause.

J.P. was unwell on the 8th, and his doctors had ordered that he should refrain from undue physical exertion. Arriving at the Congress *maidan* J.P. was amazed at the number of people who had opted to join the march. The *satyagrahis* wore saffron headbands, and the Shanti Sena cat on their arms. At four o'clock, the long, sinuous procession winded out of the *maidan*, with J.P. in the Landrover at the head. Behind him, walking, was a knot of women *satyagrahis*, and bringing up the rear a police van on the pretext of security. The marchers walked with their hands behind their backs, all of them silent—whatever they had to say was painted on card-board placards held aloft by the marchers themselves; these proclaimed the peaceful, non-violent nature of the march, and its condemnation of Government ineptitude, corruption, rising prices, unemployment and police atrocities.

Thousands joined the ten-kilometre march through the city and many more thousands lined the streets to catch a glimpse of their beloved leader and to murmur their encouragement to the *satyagrahis*. There was not a single slogan or shout—in keeping with the spirit of a silent procession, the crowds signifi-ed their support by clapping.

After three and a half hours, the column arrived at Congress *maidan* once more, its ranks swelled by many thousands more. Still in mourning for Bihar and the entire nation, the people dispersed silently, without a word.

The next day, at five in the evening, another giant gather-ing, this time at Gandhi *maidan*. At least 1,50,000 people were present, but this time they had not been asked to keep silent. As J.P. threaded his way to a makeshift platform the crowd swelled and jostled, and great shouts of *Loknayak Jayaprakash Zindabad* rent the air. J.P. said : 'For 27 years I have watched events unfold, but I can stand on the sidelines no longer. I have vowed not to allow this state of things to continue. . . . ' There was now no doubting his intentions.

Towards the end of April, 1974 J.P. was to undergo an operation at Vellur. Before he left, J.P. said :

    I am leaving Patna with a heavy heart and many worries. I had hoped that I could postpone this leave-taking as long as I could. But medical opinion in Patna, Lucknow and Vellur has urged that my prostrate gland be operated immediately. . . .

I understand well how brittle the Bihar students' and people's movement is at this stage. I also am acutely aware of my huge responsibility, particularly because of the great faith which the students, young men and people have invested in me. Some of the foremost leaders of the Rajya Chhatra Sangharsh Samiti are in jail. Those who are still free, are wanted by the police, and in evading arrest, they will be unable to play too important a part in helping the movement to grow. The first phase of the movement is drawing to an end, and it is to be hoped that the groping and the searching for a way and direction will also come to an end.

On June 2, J.P. returned from Vellur to find Patna tense with excitement. In opposition to the mass meeting planned for June 5, the CPI and Congress had planned a counter-demonstration of support to the Government on the 3rd. The Congress-CPI procession bristled with arms—tribals from the Santhal parganas formed a large contingent. On being asked why he was marching, one of the tribals said : 'I don't know. I was paid five rupees, so I came.'

The next day was full of ugly incidents. To the non-violent *satyagrahis*, there was a clear warning that the State would not shrink from using its muscle to crush the movement.

On June 5, people from all parts of Bihar converged on Patna. On this day, signatures of support for the movement were to be collected as proof that the legislature and Government had forfeited the confidence of the people. They came by every means conceivable—carts, tractors, buses, boats, lorries; but a day earlier, police were ordered to stop this mass convergence on Patna. A police force cordoned off the city, and police launches patrolled the river. The State Transport buses stopped plying and peasants were mercilessly beaten, and petitions seized. A B.B.C. correspondent described Patna as an "impregnable fortress," garrisoned to the teeth.

The people's procession was scheduled to start at seven in the morning but the time was postponed to three in the afternoon to allow for more people to arrive. J.P. arrived at Gandhi *maidan* by jeep at three, and the vast crowd began to move

with him. A banner of the Chhatra Sangharsh Samiti brought
up the head of the column. This was followed by a truck bearing the petitions, signed by millions of Biharis. And like the
previous occasion, people hung from the roof tops, adding
their cheers to the hubbub of thousands of people on the
march.

The crowds approached the Vidhan Sabha buildings. Some
months before, barricades of bamboo and steel pipes had
been erected all around. A wall of armed men from the Border
Security Force stood behind the barricades, and on either
side, units of the Central Reserve Police.

J.P.'s jeep drove into the Governor's residence and the
truck with the signatures, halted behind. All round, the
marchers squatted as soon as they reached the spot. The
Governor made faint noises about conveying the "decision of
the people" to the Central Government, and the crowd rose,
and surged back to Gandhi *maidan*.

As the people milled back, the word spread that the police
had opened fire on a section of the crowd. The report was
not instantly believed—there was dismay, incredulity. And
then a van bearing some of the wounded arrived at the
maidan and the mood of the meeting darkened and grew
tense. J.P. rose and talked gravely into the microphones.
'Promise me,' he said, 'that you will not lose control and set
fire to the place. Promise me. . . .' A group of Shanti Sevaks
near the dais raised their banner aloft and shook it—it read,
in Hindi : 'We will be attacked, but we will not raise our
hands.' A great cheer of courage arose from 5,00,000 students,
and the meeting regained its calm, prepared to listen.

J.P. said :

I am putting before you a revolutionary programme. It
will not be easy for you to act out this scheme. For you will
have to be ready for sacrifice, for great hardships, you will
have to face the bullet and the *lathi* and the jail sentence
without wilting, without succumbing to cowardice or anger.
This is a revolution, friends ! It is a total revolution ! We are
not here merely to see that the Vidhan Sabha is dissolved.
That is only one milestone on our journey. But we have a long
way to go. . . . a long way. After 27 years of freedom, the
people of this country are wracked by hunger, rising prices,

corruption—nothing works without bribes. In Government offices, banks, everywhere, even for railway tickets, nothing gets done without a bribe. The people are oppressed by every kind of injustice. Our educational institutions are corrupt. The lives of thousands of young students are in ruin, they face a bleak future. The only kind of education they get is a slave-education, they learn how to push a pen, that is all. And at the end of it all, they are no better than beggars. Everyday unemployment rises. The unemployment of the poor has already reached tragic proportions. The slogan *Gharibi Hatao* has been uttered, but *gharibi* mounts, the ranks of the poor are swelled. Land-ceiling laws have been enacted to help the landless, but the number of landless grows larger everyday. The small farmer is slipping into penury and ruin. . . . It is a total revolution that we want, nothing less.

Towards the end of his speech, J.P. chalked out a concrete programme of objectives : dissolution of the Assembly; paralysing the Government; refusal to pay taxes and excise: closure of schools and colleges for a year ; organising the people and helping to run organisations to meet the daily needs of the people; solving the problem of the poor and the weak; and propagating moral values in society.

As J.P. descended from the platform, a strong wind arose and blew the dust from the *maidan* into a thick haze. Very quickly, the high winds changed into a squall, the tents flapped and fell down, and the people began to run for shelter. Within minutes, the sky darkened and a rainstorm belted down. The storm had begun.

Those people who saw the events of early 1974 as part of the episodic cycle of student riots have had to make a whole new assessment of the movement in Bihar. In the first place, the role of the students has not been ephemeral, piecemeal—they have fulfilled the role of a disciplined enlightened vanguard, carrying the aims of the movement to the villages, providing the organisational impetus and teeth to public discontent, and marshalling the people's grievances into organised resistance. Secondly, despite the provocation, the movement has not erupted into violence—the anger of millions of people cannot

be curbed by a spontaneous, disorganised leadership; it has
taken discipline and courage to forge a campaign wedded to
peace and non-violence. Further, unlike the Nav Nirman
programme in Gujarat, the confrontation is not limited to a
few small, specific objectives. The struggle will not atrophy
when the Vidhan Sabha is dissolved. Total transformation is
on the cards.

Towards the end of June, a meeting of the Tarun Shanti
Sena at Allahabad decided that 'the events in Bihar presaged
the beginning of a revolution.' Bihar had risen, now the rest
of the country would follow, choosing the methods which the
situation in each State warranted. J.P. addressed a huge crowd
at Purushottamdas Tandon Park with the words : 'It has been
apparent for some time that the country will go through
another '42. A revolutionary situation is in the making, and
if the people's despair and oppression is not channelised into
organised action, a new dictatorship will emerge. I am aware
of the capacities of all the political parties, I have friends in
every party. And I know that there is no force in this country
capable of waging a violent revolution. At best, a sporadic
violence will ensue, it will be met with repression, and a
stronger totalitarian State will emerge. In this situation of
despair, unrest and strangulation, the students have found a
way. A constructive programme will emerge out of their
struggle. A total revolution will emerge. But not by making
long speeches from the platform. And therefore I say to these
students : come out and prepare for work. Gandhiji had
asked the people to non-cooperate. I say give me just one
year. If you cannot give up one year then nothing can
happen. . . .'

On the 28th June, J.P. visited interned students at the Patna
Central Jail. Their number had swelled since the agitation to
dissolve the Vidhan Sabha. The same day, a committee of 13
was formed to implement the programme hammered out at
the All-India Youth Conference at Allahabad. The movement,
he said, had to percolate into the poorest village in Bihar
before it could claim support. The next step was to take the
struggle to the village panchayat level, and form Jan Sangharsh
Samitis (people's struggle committees) as the organisational
spearhead of revolutionary action.

On July 8, J.P. reached Paonar Ashram for talks with Vinoba. Hitherto Vinoba had refrained from commenting on the Bihar movement—he was perhaps distrustful of the overtly political form of the struggle, and its challenge to constituted authority. J.P. went to Paonar because, in his own mind, he had not forsaken Gandhi or his tenets—according to his own lights he was making *gram swarajya* possible. Would Vinoba listen ? Would he reach beyond his own spiritual preoccupation and accept the movement as a striving after a good society ? The question loomed large for J.P.—the entire Gandhian camp stood poised between acceptance and dismay.

Before his first session with Vinoba, J.P. talked at length to the Sarva Seva Sangh workers, explaining the sweep and purpose of the movement. At 11.30 a.m., he met Vinoba, and they talked of personal matters; at two in the afternoon, they conferred about the movement at length. Three and a quarter hours later, J.P. emerged with a grim face. He was asked about the meeting.

'Vinoba asked me not to make a principle of dissolution of the Vidhan Sabha. I asked him if he thought that the Vidhan Sabha was a true representative body ?' That was all he said, but it was apparent that the discussions had not gone smoothly.

The next day, J.P. went to Vinoba again. He explained that dissolution of the Vidhan Sabha was not a principle of the movement. It had emerged as an objective out of the concrete situation. Vinoba insisted that J.P. give up this principle, and refrain from making the movement into an all-India struggle. J.P. replied that the people would decide. If the Vidhan Sabha was a useless organ, what was the good of paying lip-service to such a body ?

The next day the managing committee of the Sangh was called into session to discuss the movement. Vinoba said: ' I want unanimity. Whatever you decide unanimously, I will accept ! At the end of the first day of the meeting, no resolution had been passed.

The next day, J.P. had another long talk with Vinoba that lasted three hours. Once again, they were unable to agree.

The managing committee continued to discuss the struggle. Of 24 members, 21 were in favour of joining the movement.

Three others stubbornly refused to record their assent and repeated Vinoba's objectives at every point : a change of Government will not bring down prices—what had come of the Gujarat movement ?—the answer to the present situation was to sit down and think of solutions, not to march on the streets—and in this fashion, they questioned the assumptions of the Bihar struggle. Faint memories of J.P.'s socialist past stirred in the minds of these Sarvodaya workers, and they attributed the present course to traces of this political allegiance. J.P. wanted to transform Sarvodaya into a revolutionary body. Vinoba, on the other hand, remained utterly distrustful of institutions and organised bodies. Many times in the past, he had sought to disband the Sarvodaya institutions in order to find new sources of volition and energy, to avoid the ossification of office. And now, was it likely that his ideas could encompass a movement launched in the pith of the political process ? A silent pall hung over the proceedings at Wardha where the meetings continued.

At Wardha on June 11, five hundred Sangh workers voiced their support for J.P.'s movement. This was the beginning of the tide. At Paonar, J.P. said, 'Friends ! You must pass a resolution, any resolution. Even if it is only to condemn us. . . .'

The same night, an open meeting was held. Midway through the proceedings, two of the dissidents who did not vote in favour of J.P. offered to resign from the managing committee. The next day, they went to Vinoba and said they wanted to resign because they 'agreed to disagree'. Vinoba was stunned. He called everyone in front of him and said :

After *gramdan* I had placed before you a more feasible programme of *gramdan,* a compromise. Now, in the same manner, I place before you a concept of a compromise Sarva Seva Sangh. I have thought about its utility. J.P. met me yesterday, and we talked at length. We talked of spiritual matters and we talked of work. He said to me, '*Baba,* you have said that even though disagreements arise, our hearts should be one ! How can we remain united in our hearts ?' I will answer this question now. . . .

This is the plan I have. All the members of the Sangh, be they members, representatives, *loksevaks,* are free to choose their own fields of work—they may decide to work for *gramdan* or *gram swarajya*, or they may opt for J.P.'s revolutionary movement, but let them decide of their own individual free will. I would like them to bear in mind three things—*satya* (truth), *ahimsa* (non-violence) and *samyam* (restraint). So let there be two ways of Sarvodaya, with each man free to chart his own course. . . . There is no need for resignations. If anyone asks you why you are working in the movement instead of being engaged in *gram-dan*, then reply that 'our hearts are one and our tasks are different.'

After a pause, he turned to J.P. and asked, 'Well, Jaya-prakash, is this a just settlement ?'

'Completely'.

The Revolution in Bihar is in progress; there can be no summing up of J.P.'s life nor of the movement which he has inspired and led before it has run its course. There is a sense, however, in which the Revolution will not easily be judged to have failed or succeeded—for it does not seek the tangible goals of power or office, nor a conventional political victory, but an awakening of the people—a new Man. Towards this end J.P.'s life has been a *jaya-yatra*, a journey towards victory.

for grandeur or grandomania, or they may opt for J.P.'s revolutionary movement, but let them decide of their own individual free will. I would like them to bear in mind three things—satya (truth), ahimsa (non-violence), and sanyam (restraint). So let there be two ways of everyday, with each man free to chart his own course. . . . There is no need for resignations. If anyone asks you why you are working in the movement instead of being engaged in prayer, then reply that 'our hearts are one and our tasks are different.'

After a pause he turned to J.P. and asked, 'Well, Jaya-prakash, is this a just settlement?'

'Completely.'

The Revolution in Bihar is in progress; there can be no summing up of J.P.'s life nor of the movement which he has inspired and led before it has run its course. There is a sense, however, in which the Revolution will not easily be judged to have failed or succeeded—for it does not seek the tangible goals of power or office, nor a conventional political victory, but an awakening of the people—a new Man. Towards this end J.P.'s life has been a free-going, a journey towards victory.